Trevor Pateman

I Have Done This In Secret

degree zero

First published 2018 by **degree zero**
Unit 10, 91 Western Road
Brighton BN1 2NW, England
degreezeropublisher@gmail.com

ISBN 978-0-9935879-5-5

2 4 6 5 3 1

A CIP catalogue record for this book is available
from the British Library

Printed and Bound by CPI Group (UK) Ltd, Croydon CR0 4YY

FSC
www.fsc.org
MIX
Paper from
responsible sources
FSC® C013604

I Have Done
This In Secret

One

9.2.55   79 Lincoln RD Slade green
Erith Kent

Dear Mumma thank you for the
Presnt But now you cannot Bye me
them but I have about five pound
saved for you in the Bank I Love you
very much but I wish Dadda would
be better to us I have don this in
secret

love from trevor To dear Mumma

9.2.55   79 Lincoln RD Slade green
Erith Kent

Dear mumma I love you very much
Nowbody is like you I wish you had
a bit more money I rote this while I
was round delma I wish dadda
would give you your wages I love
you so much that I would not leav
you

Love from trevor

IT was quite recently that I found these letters, written when I was seven. They were folded into small squares, tucked down inside a recycled brown envelope marked *This One* among the disorganised papers I inherited when my mother died in 1978; she was seventy one, the age I am now. I keep family papers but hadn't really studied them; I was reading some to give a more accurate chronology to events in my childhood. That is how the letters were found.

I know what they are about and have known that explicitly since the age of eleven or twelve, but the chronology of my early life has always been confused by blanks in my memories and the events referred to in the letters had merged with earlier ones which happened at three or four years old and for which there is less documentary evidence.

Until the middle of 1955 I lived at 79 Lincoln Road, Slade Green, Erith, Kent - the address line on the letters. I lived there with my mother and father, their only child born in July 1947 when my mother was forty and my father thirty four. But there were two occasions, two long periods, when I was cared for and probably slept just round the corner, where my mother's older sister Nellie lived with her husband Ben in the bungalow *Delma* in Howbury Lane. In the 1920s Nellie won a *Daily Mirror* naming competition to which a significant cash prize attached and the bungalow built in the 1930s was given the same name. It is still there on Streetview but where once there was a front garden with wallflowers and hollyhocks, nasturtiums and stocks, roses and forget me nots, now there is hardstanding for vehicles. In Lincoln Road, every front garden has suffered the same fate and the semi-detached houses in their standard design have been Right to Buy uglified, each in its own way.

Benjamin Streeton had been a shop-floor gas turbine engineer at Fraser's of Erith and part of the labour aristocracy of the time. Born in 1894, the son of a bricklayer's labourer, he served a proper apprenticeship and had at home the masterpieces in brass which showed what he could do. But at the end of the Second World War he was obliged to retire prematurely, forced out by tuberculosis. He was nursed at home and, in recovery, made some kind of living from hand-crafting and selling, to neighbours and relatives, fine leather handbags and purses. When he was ill in bed, I sang to him *Wallflowers, wallflowers, growing up so high* ... and later he taught me simple leatherwork in his lean-to workshop. What mattered most to me were the soft skin skivers with which you lined your bags and purses, the skivers marbled in blues and pinks and violets. I later discovered that the end papers of old books were marbled in the same way. Nellie in her mid-fifties eventually went out to work part-time in a little paper bag factory at the top of Lincoln Road, and I stood beside her as she sat gathering and counting pink and white candy striped bags tumbling out of a machine which made conversation impossible, bang and shudder as it cut folded glued and spewed them. Nellie was familiar with paper sorting and counting; as a young woman in the First World War she had done the job in the big Horton Kirby paper mill on the river Darenth where my mother also became a mill girl as soon as she left school in 1921, just before or just after her fourteenth birthday. She cycled to work while it was still dark, her lunch in the handlebar basket. There were glow worms in the hedgerows.

Nellie and Ben were available to care for me when it was needed. Nellie had no children, *she couldn't hold the babies* my mother said, but she had fostered informally more than once before she cared for me. She and Ben had two Scottie dogs whose names I forget because I never took to dogs. Cats were different and in Lincoln Road my mother had Tibbles, an elderly Persian who appropriated the south-facing front room, the unused parlour, as her own. That room also contained an unplayed upright piano, a dining table with four chairs, and the family bible, a doorstop in black with brass clasps and recording mostly Victorian births and their later marriages and deaths.

When I was three or four - the only documents are some undated photographs which show my mother thin and worried and me much the same - my mother had a hysterectomy which in those days meant not only time in hospital but a stay in a post-operative nursing home and children visited neither hospitals or nursing homes. So far as I was concerned, she just disappeared and perhaps in a way which was unexplained to me. I have no memory of her going away or coming back. I have some sense that it was during this period before I went to school that I spent more time with my father, going with him to his work.

He had upholstery workrooms over a shoe shop in Lowfield Street, Dartford, where Viktor a Polish refugee worked for him. He had set up this business when he was demobbed at the end of the war, using money saved – everyone saved in the war, there was full employment and nothing to buy. I recall the shoe shop and the men in brown aprons being kind to me, and upstairs the smells and paraphernalia of the workrooms and Viktor, also kind. My father had no training in upholstery and though on my birth certificate he is described as *Upholsterer (Masterman)* that is no doubt because he employed Viktor as his journeyman, not to acknowledge a completed apprenticeship.

Starting out in business with the workrooms, my father soon added two nearby lock-up shops in Ripley's Market and Kent Road, selling carpets and linos. In the evenings he went out to lay what had been sold in the shops. He employed Mrs Wicks at Ripley's and a visit to her market shop meant walking past the horse meat butchers, split down the middle carcasses hook hanging from the walls. The internet tells me that Ripley's Market is now derelict and closed off from Lowfield Street, awaiting demolition.

Mrs Mardell managed Kent Road and she and her husband were my godparents, but God knows why – I never got to know them or why they were picked for the job required by my Anglican christening. They were handed small cards to remind them of the promises I made through them acting on my behalf, since at one month old I was not able to commit with my own words *To renounce the devil and all his works, the vain pomp and glory of the world, with all covetous desires of the same, and the carnal desires of the flesh.* I'm told that the words haven't changed much since 1947.

Before the war, my father had worked for Potts of Dartford, an old-fashioned department store, and on their 1938 marriage certificate he is described as a salesman and my mother as having no occupation. Aged thirty one, she was no longer working in the paper mill but had become the youngest child still living at home and caring for a widowed and frail mother. She met my father when he came to the door on business from Potts.

I think of my father at this period of my childhood as a carpet layer rather than salesman or upholsterer and in later life his hands were evidence for his past occupation: the constant use of stretching tools when laying old-fashioned wool carpet, using the palm of your hand as a sort of hammer, damaged tendons and my father's fingers eventually curled into the palms of his hands. In addition, there were the mis-shapen finger joints from the times when instead of hitting a carpet tack with the thin tack hammer you instead hit the finger which held it. In those days, it was not something with which to trouble Accident & Emergency; you let the bone re-set itself. I have never thought of A & E as something to make use of; it was somewhere you might get taken if you collapsed but not somewhere you took yourself. Without telephones or cars it was not very practical anyway, and when as small children my playmate David and I hurled stones at each other across Lincoln Road, it was dealt with at the kitchen sink when one of his sliced my upper lip. His effort is still marked by a scar. I took myself to A & E for the first time when I was in my sixties and even then delayed, causing further damage from the problem which forced me there.

I saw my father's workshop and his shops; there were also trips to the east end of London, to the carpet warehouses off the Commercial Road, vast and cavern-ous, the enormous rolls of carpets piled and cascading, a perfect soft play space. The highlights of the journey were the drives through the Blackwall Tunnel, an echo cham-ber for the screeching produced continuously by vehicle tyres as they made contact with the invisible kerbs keeping you away from collision with the walls. Vehicles travelled both ways in the narrow tunnel - the second tunnel was not opened until 1967 - and buses of necessity had to hug those kerbs.

My father's success was established when he acquired a new van. One evening in Lincoln Road, and completely out of the normal course, my mother woke me from my bed, took me downstairs and out into the night road to inspect a brand new Morris van PKM 672 painted green and yellow with traditional lettering *A. G. PATEMAN – CARPETS & LINOS – Dartford 4691*. I climbed into the empty paint-fresh interior. This was also when I was three or four.

*

The hysterectomy was my fault though it was a price worth paying. It's a complicated story and I got it in instalments. I have a feeling that I put two and two together and made five long before I could formulate it all explicitly.

My mother's labour was long and painful but at the end there was me, and I was God's forgiveness. God had allowed her to have a child at an age when she did not expect to have one and God anyway had several reasons for denying her. She had become pregnant shortly after her marriage, miscarried, thought nothing of it, and went to the cinema the same evening. Soon pregnant again, she felt ambivalent. I don't know why; she may have done a re-take on the miscarriage and seen it as a sign of God's unhappiness with her. There is a bit of evidence that she felt in some way unworthy and that the baby would bear the mark of that, a cursed child. But, anyway, she tried the folk remedies, gin and hot baths, to no avail it seemed. She went into labour in the county hospital, the old Dartford Union Workhouse, where Sister Gantry delivered Elizabeth who would have been my older sister. But Elizabeth was stillborn and removed for burial; in the hospital grounds, according to Sister Gantry. My mother was not entirely surprised: as she walked into the hospital accompanied by her sister in law Lena she told her, *This baby's dead. I can feel it cold inside me* and she later told me too. She used the word *septicaemia* to characterise the initial consequence of the still birth, but I don't know whether she meant by the word what is now meant. She was placed in a room by herself where, secretly, she threw her meals out of the window. Her husband had to be nudged by in-laws into visiting. He was staying away, perhaps because he was incapable of relating to what had happened to his wife; perhaps because he was demonstrating displeasure at being let down and inconvenienced. I don't really know but, unfortunately, both are plausible narratives.

Sister Gantry wrote out a poem which my mother kept and on the reverse she has written in her neat, upright hand *Sister Gantry of West Hill Hospital wrote this when I lost my Little Girl*:

> *When God takes a little child we weep*
> *and wonder why*
> *Why it should be born, to live, to suffer and to die.*
> *The lonely mother in her sorrow is too blind*
> *to see*
> *How rich in real experiences and glorified with grief.*
> *The keeper of a little life so innocent so brief*
> *A bud a thing of beauty in this world*
> *of war and vice*
> *God plucked it, and planted it, somewhere in paradise*
> *To bloom in his own garden*
> *Saved from sin and power*
> *Till he gives it back to her*
> *A fair and more perfect flower*

There is no alternative transcription which would improve it. Google returns only one result if I put in quotes the words *When God takes a little child*.... A character in the best-selling *East Lynne* by Victorian novelist Mrs Henry Wood uses them and adds *it is because He loves him.* The passage is decorated with flower imagery. My mother thought of heaven as a garden, though not often as a garden she would ever experience. For much of her life, certainly after the still birth and possibly before, she believed herself damned, a belief which when active kept her away from churches which are intended for the saved. My mother's belief in my birth as God's forgiveness proved to be temporary. It had not washed her clean of sin and so her church attendance was irregular. She read her Old and New testaments at home, a religious sect of one. As a teenager, I gave her as birthday presents the New English Bible translations. My own experience of church and Sunday school was intermittent and almost entirely Methodist, my mother comfortable with that close-to-Anglican version of low church and a teetotal tradition to which she was sympathetic.

*

I can't remember a time when my mother did not confide in me. Nor can I remember any time when I asked for much clarification or expansion of what she said. It's not that I wasn't a curious child, just one who was unassertive. But I did listen. So when my mother spoke of *Sister Gantry* I did not ask, *Who was she?* or *Why is she important?* or *Was she really your sister?* I just assumed that she was important and that it was important to my mother that I listened attentively. The name was something she wanted me to hold in my head, that's all. It's only now, a lifetime later, that I have used the memorialised name as a search term.

When the West Hill hospital site was re-developed a

decade ago, the builder Barratt's proposed to the local council a potential list of names for the new roads. Remarkably, there are no *Jubilees* or *Meadows*. Instead, Barratt proposed to conserve the names of old hospital wards and medical staff. One of their proposals (not accepted) reads *Sister Gantry* expanded upon in the 2006 local council minutes, *She heroically saved several patients during World War Two.*

During the early hours of 5 September 1940 a high explosive bomb demolished two women's wards, killing a nurse and twenty four patients. *The Manchester Guardian* reported the incident and the fact that a Sister Gantry, regardless of her own safety, and wearing only a coat over her nightdress, crawled in and out of the wreckage with a bowl of hypodermic syringes giving injections of morphia to trapped women.

My mother never talked about this war time heroism. She may not have known of it. She only talked about what she thought of as Sister Gantry's kindness. She also talked about what happened next, the instalments stretching into my teenage years. In the very recent past, a much older surviving cousin of mine corroborated some details, through the intermediary of his daughter doing a family genealogy.

*

After the stillbirth, my mother fell into a deep depression, blaming herself in terms largely framed by the punitive Christianity she had got from her mother. One day, she went into the outdoor toilet of her mother's house where she was living with her new husband and using one of his lino knives, cut her throat. She was a country girl and did not realise that *throat* in this context is really *jugular*, at the sides not the base, and stabbed into her throat. She was found by her sister Winnie who exclaimed, *You wicked girl!* There followed removal to Stone House hospital, just outside Dartford, originally built as the City of London Lunatic Asylum. Later in life, my mother often wore high-necked jumpers or choker necklaces to hide her scars.

Attempted suicide was a grievous sin in the Christian book to which my mother and her own mother born in 1867 and the sister Winnie subscribed, and it was a criminal offence in England until 1961 though prosecutions had ceased. It had once been a capital offence and I read that in the nineteenth century, failed suicides were sometimes prosecuted and condemned to be hanged by the neck until dead. In England by 1939, hospitalisation would lift any vague threat of prosecution. In my mother's case, I doubt that removal to an asylum had any therapeutic dimensions whatsoever. Sister Gantry told her that God had taken her child, Winnie had declared her wicked, her husband had shunned her, and her sister in law Lena was a Ward Matron at Stone who gave her a broom and told her to sweep the floors. Where is the comfort? So I do not find it surprising that this hospitalisation was just the beginning of my mother's career as a mental hospital patient.

*

This chapter - opened and closed before I was born, with the War as another chapter in between - became part of the way I defined myself. There is a school exercise book of English compositions and when I turn to the page dated 16th September 1957, I find that my class teacher, Mr Brown, has set the title *An Autobiography*, no doubt to find out a bit about his new top year pupils who he has to prepare for the Eleven Plus. My ten year old self opens his life like this:

> *I was born on the 19th of July '47 At The West Hill Hospital Dartford To my mother, who would have had a girl, but it died at birth.*

My mother at forty was at the very least relieved to have a live child and perhaps *Boy* was better than *Girl* because it was then not a reminder of the past. I don't know how old I was when my mother used those words *God's forgiveness* to me, casting me in the role of his begotten son, and an only one too. But I had already discovered the narrative before it was formulated. If my father felt excluded, it was not just what happened later in the mother-son duet which triggered that feeling; it was there at the beginning. My birth was between the mother and God; the father wasn't involved. *I was born ... To my mother ...*

There are in my country many grown up women who remember that they were or they weren't Mary. No man remembers being or not being Joseph. He's not the father and he can't even get his act together to organise a room at the inn. He's a spare prick at someone else's big occasion.

My father was pleased to have a son, even if I disappointed him by being the wrong sort of Son. I don't recall him ever praising me, perhaps you don't recall that since praise, I now observe, comes in bucketloads in many young children's lives. But unlike Joseph, who didn't have a cat's hope anyway, my father did everything possible to make me align myself with my mother and distance myself from him. I don't think I was initially hostile and I have already sketched time spent with him in his work environments, more so than many young children. But the problem remains that from the time of my very earliest memories, he is an aggressor and the object of his aggression my mother. From when I was three or four, this:

We are in the back living room at Lincoln Road. There is a coal fire and my father is arguing with my mother about who should poke it. He seizes the poker from her and she falls backwards into her chair, hurting her back which was a source of problems anyway, causing her to wear a surgical corset. I am distressed. My father takes my hand and pulls me unwillingly out through the kitchen and into the garden to feed a pet rabbit which is nameless in my memory. I resist. I want to be indoors with my mother.

Poking the fire. It's cheap metaphor but there are hidden aspects to this memory which I did not see until much later. There is my mother's stubbornness; she would not budge and I came in due course to feel how frustrating that can be. As a result, and as stubborn people do, she always lived worse than she could have done. There is something else happening which in the past I also overlooked. When things get out of control and my mother is hurt, my father does not come out of marital conflict mode, apologise and seek to comfort his wife. He leaves her to sort herself out, removing himself and me from the scene. I don't think my father was capable at all of apologising or comforting; it was out of his range. He only gave when he was in a very good mood, and the thing of all things which came easiest to him was to withhold, whether affection or money. And that meant, among other things, that giving comfort was left to me and as I read them it is one of the things I am trying to offer in the two letters with which I started. In fact, I am offering everything I can think of: love, loyalty, money, and the clearest of clear statements that I see my father as a wrong-doer.

I don't want to make excuses for my father though I have no doubt that his own childhood was wretched. He never, ever spoke about it, even in outline: where he lived (which was in Dartford though he was born in north London), which local schools he attended, how he got his first job. On the other hand, he seemed to have reasonable relations with his two sisters and his brother, all of whom lived locally, and with his parents who, unlike my mother's parents, were alive and also living nearby. They used to come to us for a Christmas lunch which my mother cooked.

*

As part of the oral history of our families which she conveyed to me, bit by bit, my mother would do my father's family history as best she could, but there were lacunae. She did not know the first names of my paternal grandmother or grandfather who always called each other *Mum* and *Dad*. Occasionally, I was taken to their home. I remember the address - 41 Churchfield Road, Welling - and so I streetviewed it to confirm that it is a Victorian house at the end of a terrace (and not of the meanest sort) and with a side garden which still extends to the end of the road. Welling was then supposedly in Kent but really it's part of London's south easterly sprawl.

We never entered by the front but went round the side, unannounced, and in by the kitchen door. The garden was overgrown with just a damson tree and a brick outhouse toilet furnished with torn up squares of newspaper. The kitchen is dark in my mind but very clear is the deep sink by the kitchen window and the one brass tap with a filthy rag hung over it. From that kitchen you stepped into the living room, the big furniture including a square dining table with chenille cloth covering and a long sideboard. By the fireplace at the end of the room there was an armchair and my grandfather sat there. I called him Grandad and his wife I called Grandma. They were born in 1885 and 1886, so they were both in their sixties in my early childhood and that surprises me; I thought they were very old.

Grandad sat by the fireplace pushing uncut logs into the fire. In my memory, this is his permanent occupation. Grandma was often standing up, providing tea and biscuits. My mother took the view that Grandad and Grandma lived on tea and biscuits and sardines on toast. I think this may have been close to the truth, though Grandma also had great faith in Guinness.

On one or two rare occasions I got as far as the hallway and front room but the upper floor, accessed by an uncarpeted stairway, was out of bounds. It could have housed two bedrooms and a bathroom, but the latter is doubtful. In my view, my grandparents never took a bath and, at most, would have taken a strip wash at the kitchen sink after boiling a kettle of water on the gas stove. There was, of course, no washing machine, no refrigerator, no telephone and no television.

The large front room, with bay windows looking out onto the street, was full of boxes and bric à brac. My grandmother was a great frequenter of church jumble sales and clearly had an eye for Victoriana with which she had filled her unused parlour. She would occasionally gift or sell an item to my mother and I still have knick-knacks which I think of as from Grandma's house.

My grandfather would address me from his armchair and on one occasion told me about his boyhood riding in a carriage to some private school, a box of chocolates on his lap. The school was located somewhere on the south coast, on chalk cliffs overlooking the channel. Later, when I lived on the south coast, I guessed that he might have taken Roedean (a girls' school) as his model, perhaps from a charabanc outing to Brighton. The story was fantasy as I suspect I realised even as a child. He was born in London's East End in circumstances sufficiently deprived to make it difficult to track him through the censuses. On my parents' wedding certificate he is described as a school caretaker, but my mother said he was a bookie's runner, an occupation which could easily have run alongside his official employment. School caretakers didn't take care. They usually made themselves a snug somewhere where they could read the newspaper and smoke. Nonetheless, he was given to wearing battered three piece suits and a silver watch on a gold chain, both of which I eventually inherited because I was the last in this line of Patemans. My father's older brother had two daughters. He was a *William* who was always called *Willy*; my father an *Albert* who was never, but never, called *Bert*. Anyway, I'm still the last stop on this Pateman line since I also have two daughters.

My grandfather, Albert William Pateman, a short man with a square head, held himself artificially erect and my mother classified him as German by descent and thus a source for my father's ill-temper. My grandmother had a remarkable non-English look including a very big nose, which led my mother to classify her as Jewish and a source for my father's meanness. As a teenager I liked to entertain the belief that I might be part German and part Jew, it made me a bit more exotic. Later, I felt obliged to discard the ideas as totally unfounded. Internet genealogy yields a grandfather descended from a line which found the squalor of London's East End preferable to the poverty of East

Anglian farmlands. It also yields an Eliza Kate Veryard as a grandmother whose printing compositor father migrated from Somerset to London. He and his Somerset wife had so many children that their descendants are all over the internet looking for each other and there is even a suggestion of past exoticism in tales of shipwrecked Spaniards and Huguenots fleeing persecution. If you had dressed her in black widow's weeds, I reckon Grandma would have Passed on either side of the Pyrenees, regions where - I discover to my surprise - crypto-Jews apparently lived as Catholics or Protestants following the expulsion of the Jews from Spain in 1492. It would be a comfort to think that my mother's oral history might carry the trace of truths which escape internet genealogy.

Grandma had a shapeless body, shapeless dresses, woolly stockings and very few teeth. My grandparents lived a shapeless life and, apart from my grandmother's enthusiasm for jumble sales, I am confident that they had no projects and, most definitely, no interest in Godliness or cleanliness. The former was an asset, thanks to which my father was God-free. These grandparents could stand as representatives of a vast urban underclass who in those days might well be found living in a substantial Victorian terrace house, totally neglected. It's possible that in their retirement they were helped out financially by Willy, a successful small businessman who had a builder's yard in Welling and specialised in constructing blue-tiled swimming pools. Eventually, he was successful enough to build one in his own back garden, and used it to breed koi carp.

*

My father had a bank account but business was mostly cash and he regularly came home to Lincoln Road with cloth bags containing the shop takings, storing them in the cupboard under the stairs. I am certain that as little as possible of this cash was declared for tax purposes. But like many small businessmen with that way of thinking, he never became wealthy and when he died his estate in Tesco shares and cash amounted to the price of a modest flat. He was living in council sheltered accommodation and the cash was kept hidden for fear of discovery by Social Services. I didn't know about it either.

The likelihood that there was cash in 79 Lincoln Road must have been fairly obvious to anyone looking at my father's van and one night we were burgled: a window forced, heavy boot marks in the ground outside, the bags taken from the cupboard together with my little pocket money purse which happened to be sitting on top of the ornamental upright piano in the adjacent parlour front room. I told my parents that I had heard something in the night.

If my mother was in favour, she got her housekeeping money. If she was out of favour, she didn't. That's how my father acted throughout his life, towards me as well as towards his wife. Just as there are some people who are better at hate than love, so my father was better at withholding than giving, far far better.

When he withheld housekeeping, he reckoned - correctly - that my mother would draw down on the savings in her wartime Post Office account to buy food and so on. She did that until one day much later - I was maybe twelve and the marriage in its terminal phase - when she refused to feed my father. I was there. My father reached into his pocket, passed me some coins, and told me to go down the local shop, buy him some bread and cheese.

The two letters show me clearly aware of the withholding at the age of seven and I am trying to help out. *I wish dadda would give you your wages* but I also offer up the five pounds in my Post Office savings bank account. Those accounts were promoted in schools through the sale of National Savings stamps which you stuck in a book and converted to a bank deposit when you got to a pound or so. For sixpence (forty to the pound), you got Princess Anne on a green background and for half a crown (two shillings and sixpence, so eight to the pound) you got Prince Charles on blue. Half a crown was the kind of sum you might hope for on a visit to a generous aunt and uncle. The savings accounts were important to governments as a source of low-interest loans. Most of the time, because of inflation, your money lost value, helping to ensure that the poor are always with us.

*

My mother has disappeared for a second time, I am very anxious and I am trying to make sense of it and I write letters. I don't ask for anything back, but I put both anxiety and diagnosis onto paper. I don't know what had been said to me to explain my mother's disappearance. I did not see her go though there is the trace memory of a black car driving away from *Delma*. I definitely do not recall her coming back. There are no letters back to me; maybe you didn't have the right of correspondence when you were in a mental hospital.

Perhaps inspired by the burglar, my mother stole money from the bags under the stairs. She suffered terrible guilt for what she had done, and the action was either part cause or part consequence of a despair which then led her into the kitchen, to kneel and to put her head in the gas oven, as women did in those days. But not having Sylvia Plath's knowledge of what else you had to do to make it work, she survived and was taken for the second time to Stone House hospital. It was now part of the National Health Service and boasted electro-convulsive therapy (ECT) to shock despair out of you; it was liberally administered and the treatment remained one of my mother's fears – but there were many fears and it was not out of proportion to others. In the forms in which she received it, ECT was an unpleasant affair. You were held or strapped down to prevent limbs from dislocating and your mouth kept open by a gag to prevent you biting your tongue. Then with electrodes connected, the shocks were administered, the precise forms of which evolved continuously from the origins of the therapy in the 1930s. Online, you can see as many black and white images of the older procedures as you may want.

When Stone was shut down a decade or so ago to be replaced by what is called *Care in the Community*, equipment no longer of any use was simply left behind. Urban explorers went into the empty hospital and took their usual photographs. Online and with no effort, I found images of the ECT machines, abandoned as if by a retreating army. But I have used a different image from Stone House on the cover of this book.

I knew nothing consciously of the story just outlined until eleven or twelve, when I learnt it officially. My father was abusing my mother in the flat where we had lived since leaving Lincoln Road in 1955. That is to say, he was shouting and she was not, just trying to hold her ground. My father never used obscenities or profanities, which may be one reason why I am relaxed about them in a society which is not. But he used a strange vocabulary which I did not fully understand but knew was meant to hurt. It included words which sounded like *moon* and *loon* and probably most of them referred to his wife's history of mental illness. As a boy in Dartford he would have known

Stone House as *the Lunatic Asylum*, then its official name, and perhaps also as *the loony bin,* an expression which the dictionaries tell me came into use when he was a boy.

During this particular argument my parents were in the living room and I was listening from the sitting room. Suddenly, my father stormed in and addressed me, shouting *You know what she did? She stuck her head in the gas oven.* My mother was distressed. Later, after he had exited the scene, she got me to sit down and told me that, yes, it was true and she would have told me when I was older. There were several things she was going to tell me when I was older, among them that she was going to leave my father in 1961 when I reached fourteen. She thought I needed a father until then. We made it to thirteen and a half.

It was probably on this occasion in 1958 or 1959 that I made a rare act of protest. There were three china ducks flying across the sitting room wall. I picked up a cushion and threw it at them, dislodging one duck which fell and broke. Many years later, my father was still displaying the ducks, one of them clearly glue-restored.

But in February 1955 aged seven and a half and still a long way to go, I am writing to my mother who is in a mental hospital after stealing money from my father and putting her head in the gas oven. I am *round Delma* because I am being looked after by Nellie and Ben. The letters say the rest.

*

At this early period, I live in an unhappy home but I am always very well behaved. What goes on behind the net curtains of a respectable home is not visible outside, where I act normally. At Northend County Primary School, I am commended for my conduct. At the end of my first year, 1952 – 53, there is this from Miss Friday, my Reception class teacher:

> *In spite of ill health, Trevor has made very good progress. All his work is characterised by great effort. Conduct – Excellent, a very reliable member of the class.*

And from Mrs Smart in 1953 – 54, this:

> <u>*Conduct*</u> *Excellent ... Trevor shows a keen interest in all school activities. I am sorry he has to leave my class.*

I did not complete the 1954 – 55 school year because we moved away and so there is no report or, at least, I do not now have one.

In school at this early period, it's possible that my only expression of inner distress is to be found in my *Sometimes careless* handwriting. Outside of school, there were panic attacks in which I found myself either unable to move or to swallow. There were night sweats and, later, frightening heart palpitations which forced me to sit down for ten or fifteen minutes, food phobias, migraines, and at eleven or twelve a very secret conviction that I was Christ, born to suffer and to save. To suffer at my mother's side and to save her. I think you could reasonably call it a curious example of Stockholm Syndrome, in which the hostage identifies with the values of the hostage-taker. I don't know how long the conviction lasted. But it's also true that I simultaneously believed that my mother was poisoning my food.

There was one intervention when I was nine or ten. My mother took me to her long-term family doctor, Dr

Harding, who knew everything about her. She told him I was highly strung. He replied *They sometimes play the best tunes* but still prescribed phenobarbitones - barbiturates - which I had to eat crushed into jam sandwiches because I was incapable of swallowing any pill, always gagged, and had done since I was a small child. I gagged on something the first time I went to Sunday school. A visit to West Hill hospital ensued and my mother told me I needed to have my tonsils removed. But no appointment letter ever appeared and I still don't know why. Perhaps I got lost in the system; perhaps there was never a problem with my tonsils, whatever happened in Sunday school the symptom of some kind of panic.

Nonetheless, in 1955 at seven years old I had a project to save my mother. In her absence, I set to work in the back garden of Lincoln Road and, with Uncle Ben's assistance, began to build her a bungalow which she could occupy on her return. Bungalows were one step up in the world from our semi-detached council house. There were bricks lying around the garden and there was an old picture frame which I turned into a window. But it had to be painted! Uncle Ben took me to Woolworth's in Woolwich, a journey which involved the excitement of trams, and I selected miniature pots of real paint. I tried out several colours, progress on the bungalow halted by my interest in colour schemes. I had a genuine interest in colour schemes. I declared that I wanted to be a house painter when I grew up.

*

I was told by my mother, as something rather remarkable, that when I started school at five years and two months I could already write my name which was a lot more than you could say for most pupils in that school. Nowadays with parents, playschools and nurseries all conspiring in the same direction, if that was all that could be pointed to, it might rather suggest some backwardness. I don't think I could read and there are no books from which I recall being read to. My mother did tell me stories which she made up and narrated when I was in the bath. They were slapstick stories and perhaps inspired by pre-war Laurel and Hardy films in which men are always climbing ladders and falling off or knocking pots of paint onto unwitting victims standing below. Curiously, a teacher in my first school found out about these stories and on Friday afternoons I was sat on the teacher's high chair at the front of the class and encouraged to tell my mother's stories or, at least, her stories in my versions. It was, I am sure, the basis of a later taste for public speaking.

Though I did not ask a lot of questions, it's true that part of me was curious and good at absorbing things. And even if there was not much to absorb, I was like a chicken pecking at the ground. (I think childhood memoirs tend to emphasise how full was the writer's life; it makes for better reading. It's not a page turner to write about aridity).

My mother and I were frequent visitors to Auntie Nellie, just round the corner, and my favourite aunt just as Ben was my favourite uncle; my mother and Nellie talked and I listened. There was no TV to distract and not even a wireless on. To save money, the lights did not go on until dusk. So I sat and listened and wasn't bored and maybe I knitted, though I never progressed past the infinite scarf. They were both interested in colours and colour co-ordination. I thought this was interesting too. My mother liked *Powder Pink* and *Powder Blue*. Auntie Nellie lived in a bungalow for which she had chosen *Cardinal Red* and *Cream* outside. But Nellie's favourite colours for clothing were *Mustard Yellow* and *Nigger Brown* which it was agreed co-ordinated well. More about the Brown in a moment.

These conversations started me into a world where it was quite normal and quite interesting to think about colours and colour schemes. My starting knowledge of colours was also a starting bit of cultural capital. No one ever suggested to me that to be interested in such things was *plus feminine* or *minus masculine* as far as my gendering was concerned, and I was never given a reason to hide or lose the interest. I am writing this six decades later in a room where the walls are newly painted in *Floral Street* which is yellow and adjoining rooms *French Green,* both carefully selected after study of a stack of up-market colour swatches and restoring, I just now realise, the colours of PKM 672.

When in my second primary school I joined the club which turned me into a stamp collector that expanded my stock of geographical and historical knowledge but also my colour vocabulary. Stamps were not just *Red*. They could be *Carmine* or *Scarlet* or *Vermilion.* I was never very good at these subtler distinctions, some of which are not about colour anyway but about inks as in *Aniline Rose*, but you could say that my basic colour-word capital was good for my age.

We think of colour words as things which can be used in two ways: as nouns which can be modified by adjectives, as in Nellie's *Mustard Yellow,* or as adjectives which can modify nouns, as in *yellow mustard.* However, this simple story is not quite adequate. Some colour words exist within stock phrases. So *Mustard Yellow* is more like one word than two and so are *Shocking Pink* and *Racing Green.* This is relevant to *Nigger Brown.* Neither my mother or my aunt would have called a person a *nigger,* of that I am sure. Nor would my father or Uncle Ben, if only because the word is American not English and in Slade Green we were not very American. So though *Nigger Brown* entered my vocabulary as a young child, the word *nigger* did not. I may have come across it first as a teenager.

In my childhood no one suggested to me that there were groups of people who should be hated as a group or distrusted as a group. There was an outsider group in Slade Green and the areas surrounding. The gypsies - pejoratively, *diddykois* though that's now really too quaint to sound pejorative; *pikeys* would be the modern equivalent and is freely used in online forum diatribes against Slade Green - the gypsies had historically camped in large numbers on the marshlands south of the Thames but were now being settled by the local authorities. They had a champion in the local Labour MP, Norman Dodds, whose autograph I collected at the Slade Green fête held to celebrate the coronation in 1953. The coronation was a very big event and I was very keen, reprimanding men digging a hole in Lincoln Road that their mess would *spoil the coronation*, an amusing story repeated back to me throughout my childhood. In the same way, I was frequently reminded that watching the funeral of George VI - my first television memory - I had asked *How can he be coffin if he's dead?*

The bungalow next door to Nellie and Ben was home to settled gypsies and if in the street my mother happened upon old Mrs Hutchingson, the grandmother, she would stop and they would chat. It was a matter of fact that the neighbours were gypsies, but not much more than that. That they kept chickens in their back yard did mean that when you were looking out into Ben and Nellie's back garden, given over to fruit trees and flower borders, you would quite often see a rat scuttling across. But rats were also part of the order of things and, as I understand it, still are.

What really mattered to my mother was the difference between *rough* and *respectable* and there is a whole book of course about the distinguishing features. But the short-read summary - and in no particular order - has it that God, the Queen, school uniform, sobriety, net curtains, a well-tended front garden, a clean body and clean speech, sexual inhibition, regular work and regular bowels placed you on the right side of the line. The last on the list was surprisingly hard to achieve on post-war diets and required Sunday morning doses of Andrews Liver Salt and we took them regularly.

The rough and the respectable seem always to be with us, even if the cast of those who busily mark their differences has changed. Where I'm reading from, it seems that often enough conflicting modern feminisms recycle very old tropes which mark out fundamental distinctions between those whose worldview is dominated by self-improving disapproval and those who don't mind a bit of rough.

*

At my first school, gypsies as representatives of the rough figured positively. The words I recall spontaneously (a variant on those which would have been taught from *English Folk-Songs for Schools*) are those of the last verse in which the lady answers the lord she has abandoned:

What care I for a silken bed,
With the sheets turned down so bravely, O.
For tonight I will sleep in an open field,
Along with the raggle-taggle gypsies, O.

It's a song in which the world is turned upside down, the respectable seeks its opposite, worldliness yields to passion, and it's the disorderly reversed image of that other childhood favourite, in which the Church of England doffs its cap to earn its keep:

> *The rich man in his castle,*
> *The poor man at his gate,*
> *God made them high and lowly,*
> *And ordered their estate.*

Oh, I realise that nowadays they leave out that verse from *All Things Bright and Beautiful* and stick with the eco-friendly bits. You have to trim with the wind if you want to hang on to the silken beds. As for folk songs which celebrate the carnal desires of the flesh, well, they are little taught now that we have only respectable schools where gypsies are sanitised into Roma. But if you have a taste for disorder, you can still guide your children and grandchildren to splendid *YouTube* performances of *The Raggle Taggle Gypsies*, a song which once upon a time all children knew.

When Nellie first had a television, she used to watch the News and found it hard. *It makes me cry*, she said. As for me, I would sit down to *Listen With Mother* – the title of the famous radio programme which was later joined by *Watch With Mother* where the string puppets Andy Pandy and Bill & Ben became household names, everything narrated to listeners and viewers in that cut-glass accent language which no longer has any native speakers. But the originals are there online and it's an odd experience to hear again those lost accents, which never impinged on the way I spoke or my parents spoke or anyone I ever knew spoke.

*

In my letters I write that *I love you so much that I would not leav you.* There is reproach in that too. My mother has left me in at least partly unexplained circumstances and I have no idea if or when (though I assume *when*) I will get her back. But I have not left her. That may be one reason why I have no recollection at all of how and when I got her back, how she behaved, how I behaved. I assume I was very wary indeed when my mother returned. But I continued to listen and to support and over time I became, even more obviously, her little husband, someone she could confide in and take into town for window shopping; someone who would fuss over her and buy carefully chosen birthday and Mother's Day presents. My father was often shut out from my life; in return he resented me, the usurper.

*

I knew something about my father's family from my mother; I knew a great deal more about her own family, really a complete history which proved generally accurate when I did the internet reconstruction. My mother's parents were dead before I was born but I know an awful lot about them, about her brothers and sisters, and farther back in time to family members dead well before the First World War.

I haven't classified it this way before, but one aspect of what I was told involved a contrast between those who were *Adventurers* and those who were *Stay at Homes*. The leading adventurer was my mother's father, Thomas Redsell Stevens, who ran away from home in 1875 at the age of fourteen, made his way to the Royal Navy dock-yards at Chatham, falsified his age to sixteen, and was taken on for an initial two years. My mother was of the view that he did not get on with his own father, a carpenter who my mother said *did the carvings* when the parish church of St Paulinus in Crayford, Kent was restored in the 1860s. On Christmas Day 1847 the carpenter had married in that church Emma Redsell, born in 1827, the daughter of a local cow keeper. My mother believed Emma Redsell to be Irish, a fact she used to explain her own father's quick temper, and which allowed me in my youth to think of myself as part Irish. The truth is, I can find no Irishness in Emma Redsell. But internet genealogy cannot take me back before 1801 and so it is still possible that in a longer view my mother was right. In this paragraph, it was her oral history which took me back as far as church restoration in the 1860s; before that I owe to the internet. But just as with her mother in law's ancestry, my mother may have known something that I still do not.

My mother's father had a brother already in the Navy, so he had someone to run away to. I have a photograph of the brothers together in Bombay, lounging in Pur-vezjee Dadabhoy's studio, and I have Thomas's campaign medal from the Egyptian campaign of 1882, and brass buttons from his naval uniforms. Only when he died in 1925 was his real age of sixty four acknowledged, on his mourning card. My mother turned eighteen the year of his death from cancer of the throat. He had always smoked a pipe.

He had left the Navy in 1887 and in 1891 married Eliza Turner, the daughter of a mill engineer who had moved from Buckinghamshire to work in the paper mills along the river Darenth. Her father came from a family of millwrights and until her marriage Eliza was a Paper Mill Worker, which is how the Census of 1891 lists her. Eliza's mother, Emma, is the main source of the strand of fear-inducing Christianity which continued through Eliza, into my mother and into me – four generations of it and there could be more. As evidence, I produce my great-grandmother Emma's inscription on the flyleaf of a New Testament given to her fourteen year old son *Godfrey Turner, A Present from his mother. March 10th 1882* followed by *Prepare to meet thy God,* double underlined.

When I showed that bible to my elder daughter recently, she thought the inscription very funny. She'd never come across a present combined with a full-on threat, a horse's head in someone's bed. For me it's no joke, and that is my misfortune, and not only mine. Worldwide, children are still presented daily with an image of God as a panoptical observer who holds a big carrot in one hand and a bigger stick in the other. It's hard to get clear of this model of parental discipline; it sticks around in our heads and glues itself to our bodies, however hard we try to escape. I have never felt washed clean of it all.

The best I can do as expression of my own theology is this: I believe that if a good God did exist, he would look now at all the misery caused in his name, and no longer wish us to believe. He would want us to wash our hands. Things haven't worked out as planned. I don't mind people's quiet personal beliefs, but to me there is something ineradicably vicious in the ever on-going and relentless efforts to shape other people's lives through organised religions, so repeatedly exposed as corrupt and cruel whatever God they claim to represent. Setting up women in the bishops' palaces or converting to Islam does not address what history records. We should know better by now.

But I can see that the fearful and frightening religion with which I became familiar was in some ways self-taught. It wasn't so much the creation of forceful preachers or teachers as of parents setting out to intimidate their children, as parents often do, simply drawing on the standard stock of fears made available by local versions of Christianity, *God is watching you, God will punish you* merely variants on *The Bogeyman will get you*. If they had lived in Ireland, the versions would probably have been even more terrifying, of the kind which James Joyce captures in *A Portrait of the Artist as a Young Man*. The women who transmitted the fear through the generations of my family – Emma, Eliza, my mother – were literate but not educated. They left school at the first opportunity and at least in my mother's and Eliza's case, they went to work. They read newspapers and the bible, maybe women's magazines too (my mother read *Woman*). They were not systematic and they did not think twice before saying things to their children.

But where there is public faith there is often also private doubt, that's perhaps the most exasperating thing. Emma's gift to her son falls open at John 20 where there is a Bible Marker, a cut out item with a 1935 date, and a slip with a handwritten note (which is probably in Eliza's hand) referencing verse 29 which awards you a gold star for blind faith:

> *Jesus saith unto him, Thomas, because thou hast seen me, thou hast believed: blessed* are *they that have not seen, and* yet *have believed.*

*

My grandmother Eliza Turner had been a stay at home who went out to work locally and marriage took her no farther away than round the corner from 3 Cooper's Cottages to 1 Coles Cottages, Shirehall Road, both on the outskirts of Dartford in what were once a group of separate villages – Sutton at Hone, Hawley, Horton Kirby. Her new husband had a job with Vickers of Crayford and worked as a gun tester at the top of Shirehall Road where the company had an open-air range which my mother simply called *the Butts*. In the First World War, German prisoners of war who had recovered from injuries at the nearby Southern military hospital were sometimes escorted up Shirehall Road to work on farms; my mother taught me the song which she and other children sang as they swung their arms, marching behind the prisoners:

> *At the Cross, At the Cross*
> *Where the Kaiser lost his Horse*
> *And the Eagle on his hat flew away*
> *He was eating German buns*
> *When he heard the British Guns*
> *And the artful little bugger ran away*

[But until I was old enough to hear such a word,
bugger was changed to *blighter*]

As a gun tester, Thomas Stevens lost an arm in an industrial accident, and that may have turned him towards drink and can only have worsened whatever bad temper he already possessed. He had a hook but it is discreetly hidden in photographs. He got drunk, officially, once a month in company of his brother and once came home with a bloater hanging from his button hole. He kept a cane on the table, forbidding talk at mealtimes and was cruel to one of his sons, Leonard. When Len was a teenager, the employer to whom he was apprenticed at the local forge came to the Stevens house and remonstrated with the father and told him that he should be proud of his son. But these were hard times for children.

When a boy in Shirehall Road was found sleep-walking outdoors, he was horse-whipped out of it.

My mother was afraid of her father. In contrast, she loved her mother unreservedly; she was the angel in the house who never uttered a cross word, the nature of her life perhaps captured in the Mowbray printed prayer which stood on her dressing table:

> *O Lord, support us all the day long of this troublous life, until the shades lengthen, and the evening comes, and the busy world is hushed, the fever of life is over, and our work done. Then, Lord, in Thy mercy, grant us safe lodging, a holy rest, and peace at last, through Jesus Christ our Lord*

Between marriage and 1907, Eliza gave birth to eight children of whom seven survived, my mother the youngest. But despite those births, Eliza was stiff with religion and her husband may have reacted against that in his drinking. Eliza had married an adventurer who had sailed the seas and the sailor, whose naval conduct record is at best average, had married into greater respectability. They were a familiar pairing, the rough and the respectable, a pairing which my mother repeated. My mother recorded her father saying as he lay dying, *You was right and I was wrong, Sis* and his wife replying, *It's too late for that.* As a teenager, I read avidly Lawrence's *Sons and Lovers* and when I re-read it for this writing, I was struck by Lawrence's careful depiction of how attraction and repulsion can be combined and can co-exist for extended periods of time, in fact, for the lifetime marriage of rough Morel and his respectable wife.

*

Two of my mother's siblings turned out to be adventurers. The oldest child, Thomas Turner Stevens, the first child to die and before I was born so he was never an uncle, had a childless marriage, ran a pub in the 1920s (*The Two Brewers* at Shoreham in Kent), then worked for his father's old munitions firm and ended up in the 1930s selling armaments in Latin America – there are photographs of him in Bolivia at the time of the Chaco War, looking the part in three piece suit and splendid fedora. At home, we had knick-knacks which he brought back.

The other adventurer was my mother's sister Blanche Evelyn Stevens who *had airs*, my mother said, and was always called Queenie. She somehow met and married a man with the anglicised name of John Ashton but who before that was Mostitian and Armenian. They left for India where he worked as an engineer on the railways and she lived as *Memsahib* sometimes wearing a sari – I have the photographs which were sent home. When the Raj ended, they retired to Birchington on the Kent coast where Uncle Jack built astonishing scale model steam trains. My mother and I visited shortly before Queenie's sudden death, and I suppose I should quote from what must be one of her last letters addressed on 20th November 1959 to her sister Nellie. I was twelve:

Hilda and Trevor came a few weeks ago, we had some laughs. Trevor is a nice boy, but I think that he is rather too confident in himself. He is clever, but I think that he realizes it. However, he will probably get over that.

The other children were all stay at homes and my mother most of all, literally at home as carer to her mother. Both my mother's parents, their seven children and eight spouses (Len married twice, the first wife lost to tuber-culosis), all died in Kent. And all were born in Kent, except I assume John Ashton. The seven Stevens children were not fecund; between them they produced just six children of whom I have always been the youngest, the last stop on another line.

*

In the summer of 1955, after my mother returned from her second confinement in Stone House hospital, we moved house.

Babyland was a new start. At the top of East Hill on the outskirts of Dartford, it was one of a small parade of shops with accommodation above on two floors, 1930s style. Today it's a kebab and googles easily because in 2013 someone was murdered there, a white-on-white customer dispute. The shop had a small forecourt used to display goods and was double fronted. At the rear was the office and out the back a toilet. There was pedestrian access along an alley and a garden adjacent. The Morris van disappeared, as did an upright black Ford Prefect which had been polished on Sundays but rarely used, both replaced by a brand new Bedford Dormobile with win-dows and sliding doors, custom painted in pink and blue but without a business name. Maybe you no longer needed that to prove business purposes to the taxman. The shop was mainly given over to prams and push-chairs with toys as a secondary line. My father could not get a franchise for the prestigious Marmet prams and rose socially no higher than Pedigree. Likewise, the local franchise for Dinky toys was held by a town centre shop, down the hill, so he stocked Corgi – and Matchbox too.

The idea, so my father told me late in life, was to give

my mother something to do. While I was at school, she could come downstairs and serve in the shop. Sometimes, when a truce had been called in the marital conflict, she did that and so did I. But there was also a succession of shop assistants, including Mrs Wicks who transferred to the shop when my father closed his town centre carpet and lino storefronts. The repair workrooms had probably been abandoned before our move and Viktor, who visited us occasionally, took over that business.

My mother was jealous of the succession of female assistants, most of them her age but one considerably younger and recently married and who (my mother confided) slept naked in bed. I acted, unasked, as my mother's spy: I would creep down the back stairs, open the sliding door a fraction and listen in to my father talking to his assistant. Mrs Wicks told my mother that her husband had made a crude pass, which she had rejected. Mrs Wicks eventually became the Helper who, in very practical terms, enabled my mother and me to make our escape from Babyland.

There was a truce called over one Christmas period – I would guess 1959 when my mother's sister Queenie died - and when the shop finally shut for the holiday my father gave my mother the takings to count. I sat with her on the floor of our sitting room and we started work. Abruptly, my mother grabbed handfuls of pound notes and confettied them into the air. I joined in. We were laughing, knowing very well that little or none of this money would trickle down to us.

But when we first moved into the new flat, there had been a sudden and, on reflection, extraordinary release of money. We had never had it so good. Perhaps my father had experienced an epiphany; perhaps he had been spoken to by a brother in law and told to mend his ways.

My mother was authorised to select paint, wallpaper and carpet to refurbish a large flat over two floors: two double bedrooms and a single, a large sitting room, a living room, kitchen and bathroom. I chose the colour scheme for my own bedroom and took an interest in the other choices. It was newly fashionable to have plain carpets, so we had plain carpets – grey throughout but maroon in my room. It was fashionable to have different wallpaper in the corners of the room, extending out say eighteen inches from the angle. So in the sitting room we had corners in maroon with a pattern but the main expanse of wall grey with white spots. A new maroon three piece suite appeared covered in *uncut moquette*. I didn't actually know what that was but it clearly meant you had come up in the world and that's really all you need to know. There was TV of the free-standing, upright box kind. A large, highly polished mahogany stereogram appeared and Hit Parade records began to join it. There was a telephone and a washing machine, but still no refrigerator. I have no idea where the money for all this came from. It was the middle of 1955. My mother was forty-eight, my father about to turn forty three, and I was going to have my eighth birthday on 19th July, an occasion of which I have no memory. There was a budgerigar, in which my mother took some interest, and in the garden a horribly neglected and still nameless white rabbit in a hutch.

In 1955 British manufactured goods had a dismal reputation, fully deserved. They had to be made fit for sale after they were delivered. Pram wheels were screwed on badly and so wobbled when turned. They had to be taken off and aligned. Then there were edges to metal fittings sharp enough to draw a child's blood and so they had to be smoothed. I watched my father do this work, sitting on a stool, the pram or push-chair mounted on a stand; it took a lot of time. I also listened to him selling. If you paid in advance for the pram you would soon want, then you got a free matching pram bag. If unfortunately something went wrong and you did not need the pram, your money would be refunded in full. *The least we can do.* Sometimes, I accompanied my father on evening deliveries in the Dormobile. He was an indefatigable talker in other people's houses but the conversations bored me. Occasionally, there might be another child of my age to make some play with.

The move to Dartford involved both gains and losses. I lost Ben and Nellie just round the corner, as did my mother, and I lost the possibility of playing in the street – Babyland was situated on a busy main road. Somehow, just the fact of living over a shop was isolating. As my parents' marriage deteriorated, I would come home from school and, entering the alley at the rear of the shops, listen out for the sound of my father shouting. My anxiety discouraged me from bringing home anyone. But school itself was a gain. York Road County Primary School, where I spent three years from eight to eleven, was a short walk away. The pupil intake was socially superior to that in Slade Green: respectable working-class and children of parents in lower middle-class white collar jobs. The school aimed to get some children through the Eleven Plus and did so, though I doubt it out-performed the proportion of available school places which determined that about a quarter of children went to grammar and the rest to technical and secondary modern schools. Even in the top stream class not everyone passed and below that stream, no one did.

But that examination was three years off when I arrived in Babyland. I made friends at school and went to their houses. I began to support Dartford Football Club which had its ground within long walking distance. I used to go with Geoff Latta and we stood on the concrete terraces and shouted as if our lives depended on Dartford winning. We invaded the pitch together when a referee made a really bad decision and remonstrated that we could *see* that it wasn't an offside. I took an interest in football statistics, especially crowd sizes which were published in our Sunday newspaper *The People*, even for small clubs like Dartford which played in the Southern League. It was one among a succession of obsessions with small facts. I began to borrow books from the public library down in the town centre, and though that may have started a bit later, I soon became an avid reader starting with Biggles, progressing to crime thrillers, and ending up - for reasons unknown to me - reading Ibsen and Strindberg plays which I had never seen. It was very much an autodidact way of reading, guided often enough by the A to Z of the library system.

I made regular Saturday visits to the stamp shop in Lowfield Street where I spent much of my pocket money. That stamp shop became the subject of national attention at the end of 1956. The elderly proprietor, George Lofts, announced to the local press that he had gone to the Dartford post office, just before it closed for the holiday, to buy stamps for the Christmas cards he was belatedly despatching. He had bought a complete sheet of two hundred and forty tuppeny stamps which in those pre-decimal days cost him two pounds. But to his amazement, he realised that the stamps were lacking their perforations. The whole sheet was imperforate. Stamp collecting was still a major hobby and an error like that was national and international news – the story ran in Singapore and the USA, I now discover. George Lofts reckoned he could sell the stamps for fifty pounds each, twelve thousand pounds for the sheet.

Unfortunately, his story was untrue. A sixteen year old trainee post office clerk had spotted the sheet in her stock, knew enough about stamp collecting to purchase it promptly for two pounds (half her week's wages), and walked it round to Mr Lofts' stamp shop. He paid her forty pounds, ten weeks' wages. When the true story very quickly came out, I don't know how, she was repri-manded (but not sacked) and gave away her forty pounds to the National Spastics Society, leaving her two pounds out of pocket. She was a Sunday school teacher and though she had not committed a crime, the Post Office protocol would have been to remove the sheet from sale so that it could be destroyed, and she may have known that. As for Mr Lofts, he was disgraced and abandoned his shop for a back office in the family removals company whose large *Geo. J Lofts* vans were familiar local sights. The valuation of the stamp was downgraded and in the Stanley Gibbons catalogue it does not get its own number, just a footnote explaining that because of the *irregularity* in the way it was obtained *we do not consider it properly issued.* But there is a bit of *schadenfreude* there; last time I looked at their sales list, Gibbons was offering a pair of the *Dartford 2d Brown* for three hundred and seventy five pounds.

*

In the teenage version of my archive, I have six single sheets of paper on which I have typed numbers in sequence 0003 – 0008. Clearly, I expected a large life-time depository to grow out of these small begin-nings which comprise half yearly reports from York Road representing my years with Mrs Clarke, Mrs Faulkner and Mr Brown who all judge me to be *Good* and *Very Good* in most subjects but declining to *Satisfactory* and *Tries* for Physical Education and Handwork.

I also have that school exercise book of English compositions, though now lacking its cover and hence its archival number. My ten year old self got a B minus for the *Autobiography*, from which I earlier quoted the first sentence and now quote the whole. The spelling and capitalisation are preserved, all originally done with classroom steel-tipped pen (we had ink-wells in our desks):

I was born on the 19th of July '47 At The West Hill Hospital Dartford To my mother, who would have had a girl, but it died at birth.

In the first five years I had very few illnesses and was quite fat. Sometimes I used to take to bed a teddy bear about 3 feet tall kangaroo and a tiny teddy bear which was my favourite. The only incidents I can remember are. I dropped a brick on my toes when I was about 4 years old. Just before or after I went to school we were coming to Dartford on the bus when the tire burst. I began to scream, but stopped very quickly. The driver drove into a lamppost to save the bus from toppling over

I started school when I was five. On the first day at school I slipped when I was going into the classroom. The name of the school was Northend C.P.S My first teacher was a Miss Friday That year I only had about one month at (~~shcool~~) school because of illnesses. I had Measles Scarlet Fever Chicken Pox Hooping cough and other things. IN The next two years nothing much happened My

*teachers were Mrs (~~Clarke~~) Smart and Mrs Cole.
In October 1955 we moved from 79 Lincoln Rd
Slade Green, Erith, to Babyland.*

*When I joined this school I went into Mrs
Clarke's class I liked her very much. I also came
second or third in the tests. When I went into Mrs
Faulkner's class I liked her but not as much as Mrs
Clarke.*

Mrs Faulkner made the mistake one day of calling me,
audibly to the class, an *Old Woman* when I went up to
her desk with some complaint, probably directed against
the girl I was sat next to. But what now strikes me is
those two years when *nothing much happened*. I had
either repressed an awful lot of memory or learnt that
there are secrets you do not write about in school essays.

Mr Brown later elicited a description of *My House* on
14th October 1957 which got a B plus and no comment:

*There are over thirty stairs and as I am running up
and down them all day, I do not put much weight
on. The exterior is different from most peoples as
it has a flat roof and it is three storeys high, this is
because it is a shop. The shop part consists of two
rooms, one large and one small the small one being
the office which has an ordinary oak desk in it.*

*As we ascend the the stairs we pass a glass panel
with a sliding door, which seperates the house from
the shop. The first room we come across is the
bathroom which still has some stock in it as there
is not enough storage room. It is unusual as the
wallpaper is green with fishes and sea shells on it.*

*Next we come to the kitchenette with living room
combined. there is a table three chairs and two*

fireside chairs. In the kitchenette part there are the usual utensils. As we leave the room we walk along a passage to the lounge this room is eighteen feet long. In it there is a three piece sweat in maroon a grey carpet and wallpaper is spotted with white in the corners (are) is a maroon wallpaper with gold streaks.

Again we ascend the stairs the first room we come across is the stock room but this has little importance. My bedroom has yellow contemporary wallpaper with a different paper in the corners. There is a natural oak bedroom sweat as well at the end of it. the roofline slopes downward but the window juts out. there is also a trap door.

Last of all comes my mother and fathers bedroom it is almost the same as mine except for the furniture and wallpaper.

I read this class essay after writing the description given earlier and am struck by the similarities. It does not escape me that this piece of schoolwork, eked out with obsessive detail, is written with complete lack of emotion. I do not like or dislike anything about *My House*. The nearest I get to the expression of feeling is to dismiss the stockroom as of little importance. In reality, these carefully described rooms were the setting for displays of marital discord which worsened further in the years to follow so that by the time my mother and I fled *Babyland*, my mother was sleeping in my bedroom, the natural oak chest of drawers pushed hard up against the door as a barricade.

I ought not to leave it at that. If I had written this memoir thirty or forty years ago, it would have read as a simple-minded feminist tract, a would-be act of solidarity with women. But in truth, a feminist tract would have been an easy way of avoiding a complicated story. You could say that I took my mother's side and that it was the right side. Or you could say that I had no choice, and that my mother should not have allowed things to get to the point where at fifty three years of age she was crying herself to sleep on the floor of my thirteen year old's bedroom.

In the same way, my father did not give me much choice. Until the last few months, when he began to drink to get up the courage to drive us out, his violence was verbal rather than physical and never directed at me. Towards me he was simply mean and made it clear that he thought me poor value; I could never satisfy him. I don't now feel uncomfortable about being *Male*, though for a long time I did, and I find the modern use of *Gender* when *Sex* is meant nothing more than the irritating consequence of bad sociology and prudishness. But my father did make it very hard for me to develop a *masculinity* with which I could feel comfortable. I have ended up with some of his minor eccentricities - he wore distinctive hats, I wear them too - but, for example, I have no access to what one might call reasonable anger. I was witness to so much anger which seemed groundless and was debilitating for both my mother and me. Nor do I have much access to an assertive sexuality, and I can locate occasions in the past where I made passes at women who were the least likely to accept them, thus sparing myself any further anxiety. When I knew I was going to become a father I very much hoped that the child would be a girl. I couldn't see myself as a role-model for a boy but reckoned I could manage it for a girl. In life, we should not expect too much consistency.

*

I passed the Eleven Plus in the summer of 1958. The results were brought into Mr Brown's classroom as a stack of brown envelopes. The envelopes were of different sizes, many small and some large, and it was explained to us that this was of no significance, which was a lie. I got one of the bigger envelopes and guessed that was good news. At lunch time I ran home and even before my mother had finished unfolding the contents exclaimed *I've passed!* and rushed to read the text which spoke of *a grammar school of your choice.* That choice was pondered. My father apparently canvassed the idea of sending me away to boarding school, an idea flatly rejected by my mother. At the other extreme was the local Dartford Grammar School for Boys, again rejected by my mother because in the streets she had heard boys from the school using bad language. Then there was a group of Direct Grant grammar schools, half-way houses to public schools, and clearly a cut above everything else on offer, but equally a mystery to my parents and me. So in the end first choice was secured by Bromley Grammar School for Boys. Bromley was a posher town than Dartford with nice shops and a Conservative Member of Parliament (Harold Macmillan, the Prime Minister no less). I think my mother simply assumed that it must be the case that boys on its unwalked streets did not swear.

I got to choose a reward for passing and in addition to a present for my eleventh birthday coming up in July. I chose a Raleigh Triumph bicycle in red and blue with white wall tyres, which my father helped me learn to ride, and a portable typewriter. But the choice of Bromley did me a lot of harm.

The school was a dozen miles away and the logistics of getting there were these: walk down the hill into Dartford town centre and wait for the 725 Greenline coach service to Bromley High Street. Get off and wait for a local bus out of the town centre and up the hill to the top of Hayes Lane and walk down to the school from there. Total journey time: over an hour each way, five times a week, longer in case of fog (still common) or cancellations or delays. In the mornings, if my mother had no money for some school expense I had to settle that day, I would have to ask my father and he would prevaricate and delay until I was at risk of not making it to the bus stop in time.

Those logistics limited me in several ways. It made for a very long day if I stayed behind after school, for whatever reason. It made it impossible to invite anyone back after school. It meant that any weekend contact with schoolmates had to be organised in advance. The journey itself was isolating since none of my school friends had been condemned to the 725 to Bromley. In winter, it could be very cold since heating on public transport had not been generally introduced. Over time, I developed a habit of solitary thinking, setting myself a topic to think about during the journey. Last but not least, Bromley was a school for boys. I simply lost contact with girls in whom at York Road I had begun to take an interest and especially in a girl who at ten years old has a splendidly sultry look in Mrs Faulkner's class photograph, next to the plain and stocky girl I was sat next to and who was the only person who ever bullied me at school. My mother wrote a letter, which was ignored, maybe because it was felt that a boy should be able to stick up for himself against a girl. But how could I do that?

It was in Mrs Faulkner's class that I had my only crush on a teacher, Miss Orpin, a student who I now imagine as a beatnik who went on CND marches but who was remarkable at the time not only for her appearance but because she allowed our class to know her first name (*Jo*) and took an interest in our playground games. So she knelt down beside the group of boys to which I belonged and we explained to her the absorbing task of propping against a wall "cigarette" cards from Brooke Bond tea packets and then trying to knock them over with a flicked card. You won the ones you knocked down. We let her try. I desperately wanted to be her Favourite, and I was not alone. Under pressure, she agreed to declare her True Love on the last day with us and did so. She had bought the class a box of chocolates and she gave tall, good-looking Graham Beach the reward of handing them out. I was devastated. But she had set off responses deeper than she would have imagined. My mother and my ageing aunts lived in dresses and frocks, often frumpish and often floral in the Soviet styles adopted by Marks and Spencer (and still going strong). They wore heels and stockings and very visible make-up, dominated by face powder, rouge and lipstick. Miss Orpin wore a baggy black jumper (a sloppy joe), black slacks and black flat shoes. She had short black hair and no make-up (though I am sure that changed at weekends). She had style and I somehow knew that. And she was young and pretty when all around me there were people I thought of as old. My tastes have remained much the same and most of my partners have eschewed skirts and conventional make-up, wore flats and jeans, were young and pretty.

*

That was in the summer of 1957. In the summer of 1958, after the Eleven Plus and the end of my time at York Road, my mother announced that she was going to take me to see a film at the Dartford *Odeon*. I already went there for Saturday morning cinema but this was different.

The Odeon was going to screen *Garden of Eden*, just granted a censor's "U" Certificate for universal release. Set in a nudist camp, it was the first commercial cinema film to feature bare breasts and naked buttocks. It (but not they) was all over the newspapers. My mother was taking me to see it because she did not want me to be *ashamed of my body*. It was watching this film that I was first aware of having an erection. A young woman walked towards the camera in a white blouse. She smiled as she unbuttoned and removed her top. That's my recollection of what aroused me. I didn't know what an erection was and I certainly wasn't going to ask my mother sitting next to me about the disturbance inside my (short) trousers.

As far back as I can remember, my mother had practised surveillance of my sexuality, seeking to produce confessions that games had been played with other children. It didn't help that when questioned, I blushed and a tell-tale red stripe appeared down the middle of my forehead. For many years I thought that my mother's inquisition reflected a Victorian belief that Sex is Dangerous – dangerous to morals and to health. Since she was born in 1907 and her own mother in 1867 her beliefs were formed in that context. When in 1971 I went off to study in Paris she warned me, *There are diseases you can catch*. That was fairly typical of the cultural capital she was still passing on. When she was dying, and needing to be shriven, she confessed to a small teenage sexual encounter which no one now would think anything of, would probably not remember, but from which she had carried a life-long burden of guilt. So that is all consistent with the Victorian theory. But later in my adult life, a different interpretation occurred to me.

She was a jealous woman who one dark evening, sometime in the year following that *Garden of Eden,* stalked her husband - with me holding her hand - to establish his infidelity. My father came out of the house he was visiting and saw us partly hidden behind a bush. We began to walk away. My father got into his van - the pink and blue Bedford Dormobile - and with the sliding door open drove slowly beside us, spitting insults. I was sufficiently troubled by this event to write a heavily disguised account of the evening as a school essay. I got the remark "Bathos" at the end of my effort – the only comment on school work I spontaneously remember. I had to look up the word to discover that it names a serious literary crime. I can't now find the essay.

I think my mother was jealous not only of her husband's possible infidelity, but also jealous of my child sexuality and fearful that it might lead me away from her. Eventually, it did. At twenty-nine I married and only then did my mother's inquisitions stop. In my twenties, they concerned sleeping arrangements in shared houses. I found some consolation for the bitterness I still feel when I read Wilfred Trotter's *Instincts of the Herd in Peace and War* (1915). Trotter was a well-known surgeon and became a Fellow of the Royal Society and physician to the King, but it's an incredibly tedious book in which there are just a few interesting paragraphs about how society or culture - the herd - installs itself *emotionally* in the minds of new members. In one of those paragraphs, he asserts that sexual jealousy directed by adults against children is a cultural universal, expressed through systematic efforts *to suppress and delay the development of any sexual interest by the young*. It is this repression which is the foundation of mental conflict and division in the child, experienced as the anxiety, guilt and inhibition which make the child amenable to herd control. Trotter had read Freud and talked to Freudians; he expresses qualified approval of

Freud's work. Trotter's line of thinking here is clearly consonant with Freud's own later generalisations in such works as *Civilisation and Its Discontents* (1930) and the radicalised version to be found in Herbert Marcuse's *Eros and Civilization* (1955). But I don't think I really acknowledged the connections to my own situation until I read Trotter's strange book.

From my time in Slade Green, I have two memories of childhood sexual exploration. They are both located outdoors in gardens along Lincoln Road. Boys in the road - I don't think this involved girls - played a game called *Highest and Lowest*. You pulled up your short trousers as high around your waist as you could and then dropped them, and your underpants, as low as you dared. I have no memory of any other part of this rather limited game, presumably designed to confirm that your own genitals were similar to those of other boys. And as a second recollection, a boy who lived a few doors away - my age or maybe a year older - invited me to inspect his young sister. The girl was entirely willing to have her pants pulled down but I don't remember her reaction when the boy explained to me that she was born with a willy but the doctor cut it off. But over sixty years later, I remember the explanation.

Between the age of seven, when I moved home, and that visit to the cinema at eleven, I have only one memory. There were several children in a large house in the neighbourhood, the eldest a girl of eleven or twelve and then three younger brothers. It was summer and a tent had been erected in their large garden. The brothers and me and maybe other boys were playing in the garden. The girl installed herself in the tent, laid on her back, and let it be known that the boys could come in, one by one, to Look. My mother had done her work well. I was too scared to take my turn and go in. So I appointed myself the Look-Out, sentinel at the entrance to the tent to raise the alarm should an adult appear. I glanced furtively through the tent flaps as each boy entered and left.

*

We fled Babyland one Saturday morning. My mother had been packing secretly for some weeks and my father's discovery of that forced forward our departure day. My mother had visited a solicitor and also the police station, where she showed her bruises. Mrs Wicks organised a removal van and provided temporary accommodation before Auntie Lena and Uncle Goff took us into their house in nearby Crayford. As I carried my bicycle down the stairs, my father came out of the shop and asked if I was leaving. I told him that I was.

My mother did not believe in divorce – I think jealousy of a potential other woman was part of it; she later told me, quite solemnly and despite the stalking, that she did not believe my father had been unfaithful, *he always wanted me*. Religious stupidity also played its part in putting a veto on a divorce which would have been better for our financial future. By default, my mother applied for a legal separation, granted in Dartford Magistrates' Court 24th February 1961, on grounds of my father's *persistent cruelty and neglect to maintain*. He was ordered to pay maintenance, four pounds a week for her and two pounds a week for me until my sixteenth birthday. That was it. But as I have underlined already, my father was a man good at withholding and he didn't pay. Why change the habits of a lifetime? My mother went to work but she was not a fit and healthy fifty three year old, and as a result of her illnesses and dismissals, responsibility for our support was eventually taken over by the National Assistance Board, later incorporated into the Ministry of Social Security. Periodically, they required my mother to go back to court to secure payment for arrears of maintenance and, if threatened there with prison (*six weeks* in a document I have), my father would pay up – in instalments. It went on for a long time. In one way or another we were living on benefits, sometimes replaced by her wages when my mother was working and by my own part-time or holiday employments.

There was a question mark over my father's future contact with me. Lena took the view that he should have none, and my mother's solicitor advanced that case. As a result, aged thirteen and a half, I was called into the witness box at Dartford Magistrates' Court. With my father in the dock opposite, I was asked whether I wanted to see him after the separation. *I don't mind*, I replied. Perhaps sensing that this was not an ideal decision-making situation, the magistrates had me taken into their retiring room and questioned me there. They asked me what I wanted to be when I grew up. I replied off the top of my head *A policeman* which seemed to fit with what they might hope for but otherwise sounds to me now like desperation. In reality, at this time I wanted to work for Stanley Gibbons, the London stamp dealers to whom I shortly after wrote expressing my career interest.

My father was granted access on alternate Sundays from 2pm to 4pm. On his subsequent application, that was increased and became 2pm to 5pm. I remember something of those alternate Sundays which punctuated two and a bit years of my life. I walked down the road to a pick-up point where my father was waiting in his van. We would go on some outing. There is a photograph of me on the river front in Gravesend, dressed in a stylish new suit and holding a cricket bat. On another occasion and at my request my father drove me up to the East End for what would be my first political demonstration. In the early 1960s, Sir Oswald Mosley was trying to make one of his periodic fascist comebacks and chose the East End where he had made his name in the 1930s. I had read that there would be anti-fascist demonstrations one Sunday and I wanted to attend. I don't think my father had any disagreement with that; he had, after all, spent five years in the army though not at the front. Called up in 1940, he was assigned to REME - the Royal Electrical and Mechanical Engineers - and tested and repaired tanks in the Devon countryside, his military base at Bovey Tracey. He rose to the rank of sergeant and left with a Good Conduct discharge.

The court orders expired on my sixteenth birthday at which date I wrote to my father, quite briefly, to refuse further contact. My father responded by visiting Bromley Grammar School - a first, I think - leaving with the Headmaster some forms for me to sign. The Head called me in and, using his desk, I signed away any claim on the National Savings Bonds held in my name. My father also wrote to me; I re-found his letter after most of this book had been written. I was looking for a short note but it's actually a long letter. I have enclosed it within section Three.

I did not see my father again until I was twenty. My first real lover persuaded me to try to repair the breach, to write and offer to meet up – an offer which was accepted. He had quite recently seen me on television, proposing a motion in a debate at the Oxford Union.

*

42 Green Walk, Crayford, was a pleasant semi-detached house built between the Wars. It had gardens front and

back, the latter steeply sloping, with an outhouse-style toilet connected to the kitchen by a short passageway and a bath in the kitchen itself, covered up when not in use. There were three bedrooms, two of which had once been occupied by Uncle Goff and Auntie Lena's now grown-up sons. It was a tied house, linked to Uncle Goff's employment at Dartford Paper Mills. Godfrey Stevens was born in 1903 and worked shifts as a gatekeeper, a job reserved for older men who could no longer manage the heavy work on the factory floor. There were three shifts: 6 to 2, 2 to 10, and 10 to 6 and if Goff was on nights then you had to move quietly about the house while he slept in the day. As he neared retirement, his employers offered him the freehold of the house but he turned it down, not wanting the expense of doing maintenance.

Auntie Lena still worked as a Ward Matron at Stone House hospital and my mother's relationship with her was always a little awkward. My mother did not like being bossed about; it triggered her own stubborn responses. I learnt from living in Lena's house that her medical knowledge was effectively zero. There were a few books in a glazed bookcase and I searched them avidly for sexual enlightenment but the maroon covered *Family Doctor*, bought in the 1930s on offer from the Rothermere newspaper, was distinctly unhelpful. When multiple patches of ringworm (a fungal infection) developed over my arms, my mother showed them to Lena and sought her medical advice. She recommended talcum powder. The ringworm lasted a long time. I also had impetigo above my lips, which went undiagnosed, untreated and made me very self-conscious.

Goff was a mild-mannered man who liked his pipe and a glass of beer by the TV but he did not always submit to his wife's will. When their first son married, Lena disapproved of the bride and refused to attend the wedding; Goff went. And despite Lena's scorn he read the *Daily Herald* (later *The Sun*) and voted Labour. Lena read *The Daily Mail* and voted Conservative. My mother did the same and when as a teenager I started to argue the case for Labour she said *You've got to have the people with money*. But when Enoch Powell was making his pitch for power, she said *I don't like Powell. We're all put on this earth together and you can't help the colour of your skin*. When women in saris began to appear in our streets, my mother on her way to the shops would say *Good Morning* to any she passed. *They must feel very lonely*, she explained.

I liked Uncle Goff and watched him polish his shoes in the kitchen. It was done dutifully and they were of the brown leather type which were regularly repaired and lasted forever. They really shone. He grew roses and soft fruit in the garden. Lena fed him prodigiously fatty meals and that, combined with the pipe and the beer, no doubt helped him die after several heart attacks before he was seventy. My mother had visited when he was confined to bed and when he died very soon after, she reported to me as a statement of interesting fact *He didn't want to die* as if that might not be true for everyone.

My mother had a taste for death bed scenes. When Ben died at seventy five, she told me that shortly before his death, he had asked for sex. Nellie said to my mother, *We hadn't done it for years, but I suppose it was all right.* She told me that her own mother had died *curled up like a little bird* but that she had not been allowed to visit her in hospital because it occurred not long after her first stay in Stone House and it was judged a danger to her mental health that she should witness her mother dying. I was also kept away from death beds and funerals, right through my childhood and even later. But I wasn't kept away from superstition and learnt that there are omens of death, among them the appearance of a robin. That has always complicated my relationship to Christmas cards.

Lena did make useful decisions in my regard. She ruled that I should not do my homework in the common living room but instead in the adjacent small sitting room, alone. With the stress of living with my father removed and somewhere to study, my school work began to improve from the low point it had reached during the period of separation. Bromley Grammar School tracked pupil progress in a printed Report Book where class position was calculated each term by adding up percentage scores in each subject studied. I held on to a place in the top stream throughout but from a high of 4th 5th and 2nd in the first year, dropped to 10th 24th and 9th in my second and in the year of separation to 21st 33rd and 6th. With thirty seven boys in the class, 33rd was a dangerous low. I had scored only 468 out of a possible 800 in the school term marked by the flight from Babyland and the subsequent court hearing. Demotions were rare but they did happen. First position in class was unobtainable; it was always occupied by my friend John Edward King who was in a league of his own. I only got past him once, at Oxford: he graduated with a congratulatory First and one university prize; I managed two. We were both products of a boys' grammar school organised around academic competition quantified in termly percentages. Leisurely public school Oxford was no match for us – though, of course, being good at unseen examinations did not make us better people, better diplomats, more skilful managers or more sensible; nor did it give us social clout.

Lena also played a part in getting me out of the house more. I was sent on holiday to stay with her son, his wife and their dog and it seems that my cousin John, a Royal Navy man living in Plymouth, had been given the task of enlightening me with the facts of life. He began by asking me if I knew what a prostitute was and I replied that I did; he then asked if I knew the facts of life and I replied that I did, which was untrue but it relieved him of his task and no more was said on the subject. I continued to rely on huddled playground talk, which eventually got me to some of the right answers, significantly helped along by a playground friend whose sister was as determined as he to work out the useful facts. I also joined the scout troop connected to the Crayford Methodist church where I attended with my mother. With the scouts, I went camping and that meant not only digging latrines but sleeping in tents with the chance of seeing other boys take off their clothes, sometimes followed by furtive play. The church also put on a disco for its own scouts and guides and I got my first kiss off that Methodist disco. I showed off my ability to do the Twist, but failed to follow up the kiss with a request for a date. And the disco was not repeated.

My mother found work as a shop assistant in nearby Bexleyheath, in the department store called Hides. She was ill-adapted to the world of work. At Christmas 1961, she came home tipsy, complaining that the other women must have put something in her orange juice at the staff Christmas do. A drink to my mother meant a small glass of sherry and, on special occasions, cherry brandy or egg flip. Very small. She had been Band of Hope temperance in her youth.

On Sunday afternoons, we took walks together, because it would give Goff and Lena some time without us. I think my mother, who was still disoriented, would have preferred to stay lodging with her brother and his wife but Lena pressed her to look for somewhere else to live. Choice in that matter was constrained by our income. We moved on early in 1962, a year after our departure from Babyland. As I tried to recall life at Green Walk, I discovered that I could not retrieve a single memory of the room in which I slept, presumably a teenager who had not yet retreated to their bedroom. I didn't own a record player.

*

As I review the previous two sections, I realise that I really say nothing about Mr and Mrs Wicks and I suspect the reason is connected to a record player. They were a working-class but home-owning couple, nearing retirement. I forget what Mr Wicks did but remember that he was a reader who kept his books in a glass fronted bookcase. He had read all of Agatha Christie and Edgar Wallace and lent me his immaculate hardback copies. Mrs Wicks was a strong woman who had recognised my mother's predicament and offered unsolicited help. She played the role of rescuer and continued to support my mother, who later spent a holiday with her and Mr Wicks. They had a grandchild, a girl my age who was visiting one day when my mother and I were also in the house. The girl took me into the front sitting room and put a disc on the record player. Then she lay on her back on the floor, put her arms behind her head and drew up her knees so that her dress fell back. When I did not respond, she got up and changed the record to Cliff Richard's *Bachelor Boy* which might easily have haunted me until my dying day, and did so for several years.

*

We moved a few miles away to 16 Sheridan Road, Lower Belvedere, Erith – administratively in Kent but next to Plumstead and Woolwich and like them just south of the Thames. It was an industrial area, with the giant red neon sign for Ford of Dagenham facing from the other side of the river and on our side the sour smells of the British Oil and Cake Mills. Despite the Clean Air Act of 1956 there were still fogs, sometimes heavy, the sound of foghorns booming from the unseen Thames. In December 1962 coming home from school I became a character in London's last pea-souper fog. My bus had stumbled as far as Erith before the driver was forced to abandon his journey and I walked the last couple of miles, a ghost with hands stretched in front of me. I went down with bronchitis, fetching up dark phlegm in quantities which seemed inexhaustible. On occasions when I was away from home and out late under an unfamiliar clear night sky, I found it strange and even alarming, so many stars, so far away. Later as a student I read Pascal and felt I was on the same side: *Le silence éternel de ces éspaces infinis m'effraye (The eternal silence of these infinite spaces strikes fear into me).*

Our new home was a flat on the ground floor of a Victorian red-brick terraced house divided in two with a shared front door and hallway and stairs leading to the upstairs flat occupied by a London docker and his wife, Mr and Mrs Gerrard, Harry and Ruby, who had no children and mostly kept themselves to themselves. The first room off the hall was quite spacious with west-facing double sash windows, making it light. This was my mother's bedroom. It had no heating – there was no electric socket. For some time it was without floor covering, but my mother had a dressing table and wardrobe. Then we were given a large carpet which Uncle Len had bloodstained when he collapsed and died and my mother later added an armchair so that she could sit by the window on sunny days.

The next room off the hall was my room until I went to university in 1965; I used it in vacations and later intermittently. It also had no heating, again because there was no electric socket, though there was an old gas lamp still supplied with gas. I lit it on a couple of occasions but did not dare risk regular use. There was no floor covering but the boards were painted. There were large windows facing east and in winter, with draughts coming through the floorboards, this room was cold with ice sometimes forming on the inside of the window panes. I had a wardrobe and built-in cupboard. I studied for my A levels in this room, sitting on a stool and using the top of a chest of drawers as my desk; if it was cold, I wore my overcoat. In this room I memorised large parts of Samuelson, my A level textbook of economics. In the first year that I slept there, I kept a scout's sheath knife under my pillow in case my father should force entry, though I had no conscious desires to kill him or sleep with my mother. When I began to shave, I did so with a safety razor, the refill blades for which were far from safe. I was uncomfortable to have them in my bedroom. I had no suicidal tendencies but was disturbed by the thought that these simple blades could so easily cause fatal damage. So I used to hide them at the back of the wardrobe to make it harder for an accident to occur.

Back in the hallway, a cupboard under the stairs was ours for storage and I whitewashed it, dating my work by scratching out an AP 62 – April 1962. My mother saw it and read the AP as my father's initials and was disturbed by what she thought might be a sign of disloyalty. But she never verbally tried to stop me or dissuade me from seeing him. He was my father.

The third door in the hallway led to the living room, a small damp room with a small window looking into the back yard. There was an electric socket allowing this room to be heated and to house a wireless. On this valve wireless and aged sixteen I heard the news of President Kennedy's assassination in November 1963. I recall this as the last time that I stood up and consciously prayed. I continued through my teens to be interested in religion, especially in the most desolate Calvinist versions which I learnt about in A level history (*The Reformation*), versions in which most of us are damned whatever we do. But I ceased to believe. There doesn't seem much point if you are pre-destined, though if that is the reason for not believing then it is also I suppose a perverse form of belief.

Kennedy's assassination was another proof that the world was a very fragile place. Before that, during the 1962 Cuban missile crisis, an eerie quietness had settled over the classrooms in Bromley Grammar School for Boys. We were listening hard into space, and so were our teachers. We were very afraid. We knew that we would only get a four minute warning. It continued like that through my teenage years. At another moment of crisis, I had gone into Christ Church meadow in Oxford, a beautiful walk which should be a simple pleasure, but instead I was alert and tensed, ready to *hear the H-bomb's thunder, echo like the crack of doom* against which fate John Brunner's peace song exhorted us, *Men and women, Stand together, Do not heed the men of war, Make your minds up now or never, Ban the bomb for evermore.*

My mother's brothers and sisters gave us a dining table and two upright chairs, two armchairs, a sideboard, and a china display cabinet. To begin with, we had newspaper on the living room floor to stop the draughts and later we were given some lino. It was after I had gone to university that my mother acquired a television. She never acquired a telephone, but there was a public booth opposite the house and, in time, she learnt to use this. But when at eighteen I collapsed with an allergic reaction to antibiotics prescribed for bronchitis, she fetched the doctor by running to his surgery. I still have to write *sulphonamides* when a medical questionnaire asks me for allergies. The experience gave me another reason for not swallowing pills; as a student I would smoke dope if offered but was reluctant to swallow anything.

A cupboard off this room was the pantry and in warm weather a bucket of cold water was placed inside to keep milk cool. A door off the living room led to the kitchen which despite lack of skill I painted and tiled soon after we moved in. I remember my disproportionate, foot-stamping frustration when tiles broke as I tried to cut them. There was a deep sink with a cold tap, a gas cooker, and a copper which used gas to heat water either for boiling clothes or for supplying hot water to a tin bath kept in the corner. I had a bath once a week. This organisation of the kitchen did not change in the sixteen years my mother lived in the flat. Outside, there was a pair of brick-built toilets, one for each of the two flats. As there was no light, after dark you took a torch.

In 1963, the Headmaster of Marlborough College, John Dancy, published a book *The Public Schools and the Future* which I read. As you do when you are an upstart teenager, I wrote to him expressing my scepticism that they had a legitimate future and in reply received an invitation to stay at Marlborough for a few days, accompanied by some fellow Bromley Grammar School sixth formers. In exchange, we were expected to accept a return visit and Charles Hicks lodged with me – he had my bed and I was on the floor in my sleeping bag. I think my home must have been a talking point, because another Marlborough boy, Redmond O'Hanlon, asked to swap with Hicks. My mother said no. We took the Marlborough boys up to London, to the East End and to Soho.

The rent was about thirty shillings (£1.50) a week and my mother now had a basic income of about five pounds a week. In addition to this weekly income from the National Assistance Board, I qualified at fifteen (the school leaving age) for allowances from Kent County Council for school uniform and a Free Dinner pass, in a different colour to everyone else's. A notice setting out the conditions of these grants was posted outside the Headmaster's study and I read it in the company of one of my classmates. He pointed to the line which indicated the maximum entitlement conditional on an income of less than £300 per year and scoffed *No one has less than that.* I didn't contradict him, nor did I let it be known that we had no television.

I worked in my school holidays, beginning properly when I reached my fifteenth birthday in July 1962 and found a summer job with the London Trustee Savings Bank in Fleet Street. I forget how much I earned though the figure of three pounds something comes to mind, a significant part of which went on commuting from Belvedere to Charing Cross.

*

I would not have been able to formulate it openly, but I knew that success at school could get me out of Sheridan Road. My mother, however, long continued to think that I would always live at home and I was making guilt-ridden visits right up until she died. I found the visits very difficult and compensated for my obvious lack of delight by tithing part of my income, starting to send home monthly cheques when still at university. It was not something novel. In the 1930s, my mother's brothers used to visit their own mother on Friday payday, each placing half a crown on the mantelpiece.

In the summer of 1962, my position in an accelerated stream at Bromley meant that I took four Ordinary level examinations - English, French, Latin and Maths - and passing them all qualified me to skip the fifth year (and all other O levels) and go into the sixth form where in 1964, shortly before my seventeenth birthday, I sat Advanced levels and passed with A grades in all three: Economics, Geography, History. I had become a trouble-maker and was told that I would never be made a prefect, but at the same time I had been assigned to the Oxbridge group. As a result, I stayed on after A levels to prepare for the university entrance examinations, finally leaving school in December 1964 with a place and scholarship at Oxford achieved for October 1965.

But I had already made my first break with home in the summer of 1964. It was my mother's *Daily Mail* and her Sunday *People* that helped get me out. *The People* and gossip at school told me that Sweden was the land of Free Love. My public self, which joined the local Labour Party on my sixteenth birthday in 1963 - so in time to canvass for Harold Wilson's victory in 1964 - knew that Sweden was the model for European social democracy. Despite all that, *The Daily Mail* reckoned Sweden a splendid holiday destination and in a special feature singled out for recommendation the privately owned Hotel Siljansborg in Rättvik. So I wrote to Fröken Arpi and with the help of a generous reference from school (which quietly overlooked my Conduct record) got a job for the whole of my summer holidays. There were minor hurdles to clear – I had to get a work visa from the Swedish Embassy and learn some Swedish which, in autodidact fashion, I attempted from a *Teach Yourself* book. There was also a major hurdle to clear: my father's opposition.

When I had written to my father in 1963 telling him I no longer wished to meet for our alternate Sunday afternoon outings, I am sure I had mixed motives. There was the obvious fact that his persistent failure to pay maintenance had increased the poverty in which we lived. I guess I was angry and frustrated to be condemned to the barrenness of Sheridan Road and the caretaking of my mother. To have one unsatisfactory parent may be regarded as a misfortune; to have two feels like someone has got it in for you. You can either submit to providence or shake your fist. The very simple combination of Sheridan Road, my mother's dependence, and my long bus journeys to Bromley, meant that I could not live anything like a normal teenage life. Going to Sweden in 1964 was intended as an attempt at something like it, though perhaps not one of the obvious ways.

I had to apply for a passport and that, since I was under eighteen, required my father's signature. I wrote enclosing the form, and he returned it, unsigned, and when I submitted it in that state, my application was refused. I had enough determination not to take that as final. I made an appointment with my mother's solicitor in Dartford, Mr Hewitt, and recall sitting there on the other side of his desk as he telephoned the Passport Office, standing up with one thumb tucked into his waistcoat, courtroom-style, berating some poor clerk with threats of recourse to the Under-Secretary unless this poor boy, whose father only paid maintenance when threatened with prison, who had effectively disowned him anyway, got his passport. That phone call cost me two guineas and I sailed a few days after my seventeenth birthday: Harwich to Esbjerg, across Denmark by a train which was loaded onto a ferry, on to Stockholm (where I bought a fashionable, pencil-slim and bright red socialist tie), and out by train to Rättvik by Lake Siljan in Dalarna.

I learnt a lot in that very traditional and well-regarded hotel, now demolished. I learnt how to address Swedish guests in the third person as required by politeness norms, so *Hur mår Grevinnan Kalling idag?* [*How is Countess Kalling today?*]. I listened to the classical pianist Gösta Jahn practise each morning at the grand piano in the drawing room, talking to himself as he played. There were guests making extended stays who talked to me. There was Dr R R Geis and his family who gave me a book *This Is Germany*. I played table tennis with the son; the internet now tells me that the father was Chief Rabbi in Baden and later a Professor of Judaism. There was an art collector or dealer, very elderly, beautifully groomed, mannered and accented, who walked in the forests around the hotel collecting mushrooms which he showed me. I think of his name as Rosenberg but I get nowhere because *Rosenberg + Art* just calls up Picasso's dealer, Paul Rosenberg, who was dead by 1964 but nonetheless looks exactly like the man with mushrooms in his hand.

One evening an American couple, the husband tall, thin and erect, a retired Colonel or more, surprised me as we stood on a terrace. Because I was British and therefore understood such things, they told me how embarrassed they were by other American tourists - this at a time when American tourists were indeed figures of fun - and how they tried to behave with more dignity. And, finally, Fröken Arpi at reception, buttonholed by a large and loud guest from the Deep South who owned a factory making women's underwear, showing Miss Arpi the catalogue of young women modelling his wares, and at the same time expounding his thoughts on inter-racial marriage, actually saying, *How would you feel about one of them touching your sister or your daughter?* and Fröken Arpi politely refusing to go along with her guest's insistent views, views which I had never heard expressed before.

I left with a good reference and gifts: a traditional Dalarna wooden horse and a book *The Warship Vasa* signed by Britt Arpi and her mother. But I had been too inhibited to take advantage of the Free Love which was offered, by one pretty blonde girl and one pretty blond boy. I regret both inhibitions. I did get to hear Sweden's most famous and long-serving (1946 - 1969) Prime Minister. On a day off, I travelled to the industrial town of Borlänge and there in the *Folketspark* sat with a dictionary in my lap listening to Tage Erlander address the large crowd.

On the train journey back from Sweden, in a crowded compartment of the old sort, two middle-aged women sat opposite me, one severely dressed, the other in the simplest nun's habit. The severe one established my nationality and, in English, told me that they were Polish. They had been to some ceremony in Sweden where her sister had collected an award, and not her first. *Even our Communists had to give her an award*, she said. Her sister said nothing and did not react as her spokesperson turned, took her sister's arm, pushed up the sleeve, and showed me the tattooed numbers. *She was in Auschwitz.* That's all I remember.

*

When I returned to England after seven weeks away, I was carrying a suitcase heavy with gifts, mostly knick-knacks for aunts and uncles. It's what you did when you had been to foreign parts, but there was also a burden of guilt for having been. Some were examples of traditional handicraft, others domestic items in contemporary Swedish designs which I liked. For my mother I brought home an expensive woven tablecloth. During my absence, I had written very long letters at least once a week and probably more often – I have the letters but don't want to read them. On my return, I noticed bruises on the back of my mother's hands. She told me she had been receiving out-patient electro-convulsive therapy for depression. My return did not relieve it.

I was now studying for the scholarship exams which were intended to take me away. As the Autumn Term progressed, my mother's condition worsened and on many evenings, instead of studying in my bedroom, I sat at the living room table with my mother behind me in her armchair. If she began to shake, to convulse, I stopped and turned to talk to her. I recall that my scalp was alive with prickling sensations and I suppose that was my own stress manifesting itself. But at the time I was worried there might be something wrong with my head. My mother had warned me of the Victorian risks of over-studying, comparable to those consequent upon mastur-bation, about which I had also been warned. Of course, I never mentioned my unease to anyone.

Christmas approached and that meant my mother and me alone together with little to do and nowhere to go. My mother cracked first and on a snow white Boxing Day 1964 I had to call an ambulance which took her to the thirty eight ward and eight hundred and fifty seat chapel known as Bexley Hospital, once the Dartford Heath

Asylum, where she became unable to speak or walk. She was treated with multiple shocks of ECT and remained there for two or three months. Meanwhile, from the beginning of January, I was commuting to London for my gap year job in Foyle's Bookshop, returning home in the evenings via the hospital and its many corridors, painted in the hospital green reckoned calming by industrial psychologists. Those corridors were home to long-stay patients who were lost in the asylum system, quite often for decades, and who spent their days wandering, the men among them heading out into the hospital grounds in search of cigarette butts from which roll-ups could be fashioned.

At Foyle's I earnt eight pounds ten shillings for a 44 hour week, no pension entitlement, one week's notice on either side, according to the *Particulars of Employment* handed to me on 4th January 1965. In London, I ate the incredibly cheap lunches at Jimmy's, a basement Greek café which everyone in Soho knew about, and in Belvedere I used the launderette.

Foyle's was another new world. I was seventeen and working with people mostly just a few years older, some just out of university and others often newly-arrived from Europe on work visas which Foyle's obtained sure in the knowledge that they would never stay long enough to acquire statutory employment rights and become a burden on the profits. There were beautiful young women and I became serially infatuated. A drama student with kohl-painted eyes; a terribly slight girl from Denmark with pageboy hair; a doctor's daughter from Wales who was going to the London School of Economics. But none of them fancied me. I was too young and gauche, no more than a schoolboy obsessed by his burdened life. I doubt my personal hygiene was that good. The doctor's daughter who accepted to spend occasional time with me said I was maudlin. But I did get invited to parties in Camden and King's Cross which went on all Saturday night and from which I walked down to Charing Cross at five in the morning - no night underground then - to catch the first train back to Belvedere. And I did join in the formation of a secret Union branch which challenged the regime of Christina Foyle and her sadistic husband, Ronald Batty.

He was the store manager. He walked the shop floors sacking people. He inspired genuine fear and on Fridays there were always people in tears, including the Danish girl who was sacked because too many foreigners had arrived in the same week. Technically, people held work permits that restricted them to employment with Foyle's. But even then I guess it was possible to work illegally. Nonetheless, I was affected by the girls in tears and I did not like the ruthless atmosphere. Nor did other people. A forceful Australian, Marius Webb, had initiated the formation of the clandestine branch of the Union of Shop Distributive and Allied Workers (USDAW). It had to be secret because Foyle's did not recognise Unions and Mr Batty would simply have sacked you. I became responsible for collecting Union dues in the building which housed the postal library. I had been put in charge of that, sending banned books to readers in the Irish Republic, assisted by the regularly updated lists of what was forbidden provided by the Irish Embassy. Ireland was still in its clerical-fascist period and my knowledge of it confined to what I had got from *A Portrait of the Artist as a Young Man,* prescribed sixth form reading which my class exercise book tells me I had found *too intellectual* though the phantasmagoria of Hell was *brilliant*. But my main task as postal librarian was to supply romantic novels to rural gentlefolk like the charming Lady Ailwyn who would telephone me to discuss which newly published books might suit.

Writing this, I realise that there was a special reason why I was affected by the young women in tears. In the fairly recent past, I had seen my mother in tears after losing her job and I held myself to blame. She had a job in the Dartford Co-op, working behind the sweet counter. I visited her there and saw her smiling in her smock. It was automatic to belong to the Union and automatic for political dues to be deducted to support the Labour Party. I berated my mother for not opting out of paying those dues. If she was a Conservative, she should opt-out – it was her right. I strutted teenage Principle. One day she was sacked and came home to Belvedere in merciless tears. She told me she had sat on the railway platform crying, missing her trains. I didn't ask if she had opted out but guiltily assumed that she had and was sacked in consequence and that it was all my fault. I still don't know if it was. Maybe she just wasn't fast enough on her feet for the job, a woman in her mid-fifties, not physically fit, much burdened, sometimes confused.

After a few months at Foyle's, I found myself a job in local government and nearer home. It was a stupid move which I have always regretted. In London, I was meeting the kind of people I should have been meeting at my age and with my aspirations. If I had stuck it out, I might even have got myself a girlfriend. Soon after I left, USDAW called an official strike for Union recognition, better pay and other things. On Saturdays I joined the picket line. The strike was wildly popular; all kinds of splendid people came up to us to say that they had once worked for Christina Foyle and could they please give a large donation. *Private Eye* did a lovely and very funny piece.

And when it was all over in July 1965 *The Daily Worker* put two pretty girl pickets on the front page, one of them the doctor's daughter.

But I had made a self-punitive move and got myself this job with the Dartford Youth Employment Bureau as a clerk. I cycled every day on my Raleigh Triumph to work in an office with four middle-aged people, three women and Mr Councer, the Youth Employment Officer. Back in 1965, the State was less determined to keep records on you. When you reached eighteen you ceased to be the responsibility of the Youth Employment Service and any local records they held on you were destroyed. One day in the Dartford bureau, I was assigned the task of weeding the files – taking out everything held on those who had passed their eighteenth birthday, carrying it all into the garden of the large Victorian house where we worked, and making a bonfire. When I got to the letter "J", I found *Jagger, Michael* a past pupil of Dartford Grammar School for Boys just up the road. His file contained the form he had filled up preparatory to his Careers interview with Mr Councer. The form asked the young Mick Jagger what he was interested in, what his hobbies were, and so on. Mr Councer had penned his comments and career suggestions at the bottom of the form which Jagger, Michael had completed. I was very tempted to keep it. I had no right; the contents were of no legitimate public interest. But it was a curiosity and it might be valuable. I burnt it along with all the rest. I think of it as my Mick Jagger Secret. But I hesitate to say I acted on principle; maybe it was no more than fear. I knew the story of the Dartford post office clerk who back in 1956 had temptation placed in her way.

There was another moment which disturbed me. One of my tasks was to issue National Insurance cards to school leavers who came in for them. One day I went out to the waiting room where a girl had arrived. She had just left school and wanted a card. There was something very odd about her. Her clothes were old fashioned, thick and woollen, though it was summer. She was wearing a hat in a style which to me was 1930s. She looked frumpish but she was fifteen. She seemed ill at ease and I reciprocated. I felt something was wrong and later I asked my colleagues for an explanation. They knew of the girl. She was apparently very clever and her school had wanted her to stay on. But her family belonged to some small Christian sect which required girls to leave school at the earliest legal age and work in family businesses until they married. The sect barred girls from all education beyond the minimum required by law. Her family were Brethren of one kind or another - Plymouth and Exclusive are the best known - and the garments which women wore signified their submission within purse-lipped and disapproving organisations. There are survivors' forums on the internet because these sects were often enough networks of abuse, emotional coercion and financial corruption, all enabled by freedom of religion which then as now provides a screen against scrutiny.

So I learnt from the Youth Employment Bureau just as I had learnt in Sweden. But now I was saving money to buy all the things on the long list of requirements sent to me by my Oxford college and designed to line the pockets of the city drapers who would sell me a mortar board, gown, white bow tie, not to mention the voluntary college scarf, tie and cuff-links. Burton's would provide the sober grey suit, and Selfridge's the laundry bag. I was going to be a scholar.

I find the chronology difficult to reconstruct, even from this teenage period. It's not old age, it's always been like this, gaps and holes everywhere. It's as if doing forgetting saves me from my own depression, it lifts a burden as ECT was supposed to do for my mother. When she was released from Bexley Hospital in the spring of 1965, her memory was in very poor shape. She had forgotten how to cook. So for her fifty-eighth birthday in May 1965 her seventeen year old son gave her a cook book. When I realised what I had done, I was ashamed. She had grown up in the First World War, helping her mother in a kitchen which served as many as nine - husband and wife, seven children - and that is where she learnt to cook. She never used scales (did not own any), had no recipes in the kitchen, and had never used a cook book in her life. I carry on the tradition, in modified form. I rarely consult a dictionary and never a thesaurus, grammar, or guide to punctuation. I suspect it's a bit of penance, a bit of loyalty to a lost cause.

*

My mother broke down completely one more time. On New Year's Day 1978, she ordered a taxi and had herself taken to the gatehouse of Bexley Hospital and asked for admission. She was seventy and once more suicidal. The hospital telephoned me, thirty and recently married, and I presented myself to a doctor who told me she was very depressed, no longer took any pleasure in reading her daily newspaper. But this time there was no ECT. The hospital withdrew her from Lentizol and Melleril and eventually replaced them with Valium. When she was released she seemed happier than I had seen her for a very long time.

But she began to complain of back pain which worsened, though she went to her doctor and was given a prescription for a new surgical corset. She bought herself a new mattress. In May of that same year her final crisis arrived with her birthday. I visited and found her in pain, distressed, and deeply jaundiced. I called out a doctor who physically removed all the medications she was taking: Aldomet, Distalgesic, Moduretic, Mogadon, Tryptizol, Valium, Vitamin B12. A few days later, her regular GP - no longer the Dr Harding of my childhood - visited her because she was too ill to go to his surgery and left her a letter, relying on me to organise the requested appointment with a hospital consultant. The sealed envelope was marked *Rather Urgent* on which basis, when I telephoned, an appointment was offered for two months' later.

My mother was obviously very ill and I overcame my wife's reluctance and we took her to our home. It was part of my new wife's job to separate my life from my mother's, and she was right to express reluctance. The back pain increased and my mother was now over-whelmed by thoughts telling her that the jaundice was due to her wickedness, thoughts which had been there from the onset of the yellowing. As a child she had been warned by her mother *If you're wicked, you'll turn yellow* and now her mother was being proved right.

It simply did not occur to me that you could go to A & E, but I got my own GP to visit on the Whitsun bank holiday Sunday. He examined her (her own doctor had not), diagnosed obstructive jaundice with pancreatic cancer as one possible cause, and arranged an emer-gency hospital admission where pointless surgery performed a couple of days later confirmed his provi-sional diagnosis. She died a week after the surgery and six weeks before the out-patient appointment which *Rather Urgent* had secured. I had driven her to the hospital and as I drove she held her hand against my cheek.

During his visit my own doctor had opened the other GP's letter, and passed it to me without comment:

This dear old lady, who has been suffering from chronic depressive illness & has been under the psychiatrist with several admissions as in Patient in Bexley Mental Hospital – she has been on anti-depressants, including Largactil for many years now. She developed jaundice about three weeks ago & we thought it may have been due to Largactil [a drug my mother was not taking] *etc so we stopped all drugs but the jaundice instead of lessening has deepened. I feel sure there may be some Malignancy about ? Primary – I shall be grateful for your examination & attention*

My mother would not have thought she was dying prematurely: in her book, three score and ten was at the limit of what you could reasonably expect. She had already bought a sixpenny Will from Woolworths, completing it with just the ten handwritten words required to bequeath unto *My Son Trevor John Pateman all of my worldly goods.* She would not have found it unexpected to be dying on an open ward of Orpington Hospital, high on the opiates they are generous with when it gets to this stage, the June weather fine, the doors and windows of the wartime hut open wide, sparrows skimming through. Her mother had died in the same hospital. I was away from the ward for part of her last day, torn between wanting to stay and wanting to go because there was nothing left to stay for. Blind and unable to speak, she had gestured to a nurse who understood her to be requesting pen and paper. The paper was handed to me later, covered with frantic scribbles in all directions which I could not decipher. I don't have the paper now; I think I must have allowed myself to lose it.

It was left to a woman friend who had known me since I was eighteen to comment, and not so long after my mother's death, *It must be a relief*, a thought I could never have permitted myself. For many years after, I had a recurrent anxiety dream. I had been negligent in visiting my mother and now after a long period of neglect I was trying to visit but the trains were late, the roads congested, the route in any case unclear and the dream more and more frantic until finally I would wake up in order to declare *But she's dead. You don't have to go anymore.*

Two

9 Lambarde Road Sevenoaks Kent   *19th July 1978*

Dear Age Concern

As a token of appreciation for the pleasure my late mother, Mrs Hilda Pateman, received from your Pop-In parlours at Bexleyheath and Erith, I should like to make a donation to your funds to be applied as you see fit in the running of either or both of these parlours. I therefore enclose a cheque for £27.73, being the sum paid to me from my mother's penny-a-week life assurance policy.

Yours sincerely

Trevor Pateman

*

My mother died forty years ago. At the time, I determined to memorialise her, to make something out of her life which would redeem it if only just a bit. I set the standard inevitably too high; my writing simply wasn't good enough and so I put it away, a childish thing. There is no redemption, anyway, after all the facts are in. The idea is a placebo.

Before trying to write my mother's death out of me, I had tried for justice and harried the doctors who had not even examined her as she became increasingly ill. But I have tired of justice in all forms and even more when I hear demands for justice which are flimsy masks for other things, including envy and the lust to watch someone swing. Justice is a dish best demanded hot before cold thoughts of revenge or other calculating strategies take over. Justice is over-rated and we could do with less of it. There are alternatives: dialogue, mediation, truth and reconciliation, compensation, compassion, a slap round the face. For all but the most serious crimes, I believe in statutes of limitations and more like five years than twenty five. It would help us learn to forget.

After the search for redemption and justice, I went on to read the literature on separation, on loss; on love, guilt and reparation; on good enough parenting: John Bowlby, Melanie Klein, Donald Winnicott. It helped, though it is in our nature that we read, we are enlightened, and then we forget. The lights come on and the lights go off. It's always like that. There is no more a reading cure than there is a talking cure, just the possibility of interludes of remission. The interludes may be quite long: my mother's four main episodes of mental breakdown were distributed over forty years.

*

I am ambivalent about memorialisation. As a teenager, the book which most wracked and seduced me was Thomas Hardy's *The Mayor of Casterbridge*, who does not wish to be memorialised at all but forgotten as if never existing. It appealed to my Calvinist self, and still does. But then there is a pull in the opposite direction. I began buying books independently when I was fourteen or fifteen. There was a W H Smith by the stop where I waited for the bus home from school. The first book I ever bought, half a crown's worth of self-improvement, was a slim new Penguin paperback, red and white cover, Yevtushenko's *Selected Poems*. It was 1962 and he was in the news, a Soviet dissident poet. I remember only one line, the most famous: *Over Babiy Yar, there are no memorials,* the implication that there should be. It was the beginning of an interest in the Holocaust which has been pursued through many books. But visiting Yad Vashem in 1995, I found myself uneasy. The collective memorials, the black pillars the height of which indicate the number of Jews killed in each country, moved me. I thought they were just right and they even conveyed some hope: as everyone now knows, the pillars for Bulgaria and Denmark are very short indeed because both the leaders and the people in those countries thwarted Nazi demands. But the Yad Vashem memorials to individuals made me uneasy, and when they bore the names of sponsors, I revolted. You want your name on a plaque for giving money to this, of all things?

Right now, I revolt that we are supposed to believe that the way to deal with all those men bigged up on plinths is to big up some suffragettes. That is not the answer to anything; it is part of the problem. Memorialisation is not about achieving ideological hegemony over public spaces, not least because most heroes are only local heroes and temporary ones too. All these monuments to individuals should come down; we should be satisfied with the collective ones to which we can respond each in our own way. The most important memorials to individuals are in our own memories and loyalties. The plaster cast angels drooping over old graves lose their balance, pitch over and eventually everything is bulldozed. Nobody much minds. An ugly monument to a public benefactor just as much as to a public enemy, put up by some committee of those who like to sit on committees, has no better claim to be preserved.

Not all collective memorials work; some fail. In the Soviet Union, the party line dictated that the twenty million casualties in World War Two could only be memorialised by huge and brutal installations which suggested the crushing might of Russia and the iron will of its fighters. But those memorials which lack any elements of simplicity, intimacy and privacy must surely make mourners feel awkward and confused. It could have been done differently. One day during a 1997 holiday, I walked around the National Gallery of Armenia in Yerevan. My attention was caught by a large painting (196 x 250 cm) which depicts all kinds of simple but very colourful flowers stuck in jam jars, often only a few to a jar, lined up in rows as if on shelves, some pieces of fruit also scattered around. I smiled, felt warmed, but also felt that the painting expressed some sadness. I looked at the gallery description. It told me that the painting by Martiros Saryan, dated to 1945, was a tribute to Armenians who had fought in the Red Army, both those who survived and those many who died. I was astonished and moved. I now saw the jam jars placed on simple graves with whatever flowers were to hand, and imagined the actions and feelings of those who bent to place them there. Perhaps also, the flowers could belong in the centre of kitchen tables, set to celebrate a safe homecoming. After-wards, I wondered how Saryan had got away with it, in Stalin's Soviet Union and in the year of victory itself. I still don't know and I don't know if there is an answer.

*

It does me no good to dwell on the past, the autobiography isn't therapeutic. I can't make myself do the work neces-sary to fill in more detail. At a time of life when I should be making the best of what's left, it just reminds me of the way my life has been limited. Oh, it has been in many ways a varied and interesting and privileged life which has never settled into that distinctly English middle-class compla-cency and sense of entitlement which revolved around house prices and schools riff-raff free, and which now counts its bus passes. Yes, varied and interesting but limited by anxieties, by fears, by phobias, by obsessions which come and go, though not by anything at all approaching what I think of as my mother's melancholia.

I call it melancholia rather than depression because it seems to me that the self-punishing and self-abasing religious language in which it was expressed connected to losses which involved ambivalent feelings about the object lost. One of my mother's siblings died in infancy and I know nothing about her feelings with regard to that. But she did have ambivalent feelings towards her father, who created disorder and unhappiness in his home, but died when she was seventeen and before their relationship might have resolved itself. She had ambivalent feelings about childbirth and then gave birth to a dead baby. The melancholia after the stillbirth may have had a physical component, in terms of hormonal disruption or blood disorder – *somatic* causes of melancholia, the existence of which Freud acknowledges in his 1917 essay *Mourning and Melancholia*. She had very ambivalent feelings about her husband who proved to be emotionally useless. But at some level, she never got free of him. She had ambivalent feelings about her son when he set out to leave home and in her final illness had murderous fantasies directed against the daughter in law who had taken her son away.

*

The main narrative of this book is a sort of director's cut. There is a lot which didn't make it, lying around on the desktop. Some because of the censor; some because I got bored with the story; some because I'm sure it's not every reader who is looking for bleak on bleak. I pick up a discarded cut, restore it and offer you this:

I have a fear of fainting. In fact, I have never fainted in my life. But I can point to an origin for the fear. My first school, Northend County Primary School on the road between Slade Green and Erith served an area of what we now call social deprivation. It still is deprived; the 2007 Ofsted inspection report opens as follows:

> *Northend is an average sized primary school ... It serves a community with very high levels of deprivation. The percentage of pupils eligible for free school meals is very high. The majority of pupils are of White British heritage...*

I started there in 1952 and assemblies were held in a war time hut. When we stood for prayers, children - their faces often painted with gentian violet - fainted; they regularly smacked down on the polished parquet floor. I did not know why and I was afraid. Now I do know, but I am still afraid. They were hungry; they had eaten no break-fast and possibly no dinner the night before. Some of them smelt, one of them badly enough to be called *Stinker Elizabeth* and that already in what became the unending reign of Queen Elizabeth the Second, its beginning marked by a class photograph and a china cup for every child. We will go on recording Northend as deprived until the end of recorded time. What have we changed in sixty-odd years? Very recently, we have rebranded the school. It is now *Peareswood*, entirely in keeping with our street name world of *Jubilees* and *Meadows*. There is no place in England called *Revolution Street*, not even a whiff of one.

*

I live in a very pleasant, modern, sunny and top floor apartment in one of those south coast resorts which used to be called God's waiting rooms. It's a short walk to the seafront promenade and to the pier. I live alone, of course. I worked out easily enough that of my fifty adult years - say, twenty to seventy - I lived for just seventeen with someone else, my former wife, joined for ten years by our two children. Marriage didn't suit me very well; I did not seek it and I have never recommended it to anyone. It disappoints me that so many LGBT people have adopted conservative marriage with an enthusiasm it does not deserve. Children are another matter and they go around lighting up lives without even trying. The harder trick is to find an adult relationship which remains a delight through their growing up.

In the same fifty years, two significant and sexual relationships engaged me for another fifteen or so years, but with women who never lived with me or me with them. They were good relationships, loving, playful and scandalous even, but it had been a struggle to get to that happiness and quite late in life. When my mother was dying she said in her one-liner way *I'm not going to have any more happiness* and I felt once again like that seven year old child at his wits' end. Between the boy of seven and the man of thirty stood a *youth which had seemed to teach that happiness was but the occasional episode in a general drama of pain* – the words are those with which Thomas Hardy closes *The Mayor of Casterbridge,* the thought attributed to the mayor's step-daughter, Elizabeth-Jane, who while now *forced to class herself among the fortunate* is shadowed by her past.

I know there are people who say that happiness isn't the important thing, who offer other narratives for what it is to live a good life, a life worth living. But I'm reluctant to disparage happiness even though I know that happiness writes white. I might call it contentment, but that's not so very different. Poor people want to be happy. Their dreams of happiness take many shapes and when I write that the shape which comes immediately to my mind turns out to be a 1935 Soviet film, Alexsandr Medvedkin's *Happiness,* a piece of slapstick propaganda for collectivization. It's the story of a poor peasant who is luckless and hapless but eventually proves himself a collective farm hero. It seems absurd that this film should pop up in my head. But just maybe it links me back to my mother's slapstick Laurel and Hardy stories, told to a child splashing happily in the bath. It's not such a far-fetched connection. Or perhaps the absurdity just shows that when it comes to happiness, it's each to their own version.

I am very reclusive now, don't socialise, don't have TV or radio, avoid the telephone. It's as if I want to belong to a religious sect of one. But I guess it's just the trace of things I have forgotten but which go towards making me who and what I am. I see my children and grandchildren who are all close by, but very few others at least partly because there is some inner resistance to making the effort.

It's true, I'm difficult with many of the same problems which held me back in the past, the anxieties, the obsessions, the phobias though some softened by time. My temper is better, partly because I avoid situations which might trigger it. I am most at risk when faced by the kind of meanness and withholding behaviour I endured from my father. I'm not very tolerant of stupidity either, and rue hundreds of hours spent simmering in university committees where academics flaunted their unfitness to run anything. When with early retirement at fifty I no longer had to attend them, it was like being cured of migraines, and divorce cured me of those at forty. I felt guilty about the fact, didn't tell that I was now happily migraine-free. It was like a naughty secret.

I have many opinions, as it may have struck you already, dear attentive reader, and maybe worse: I want to claim a virtue. I learnt to listen as a child and continued to listen. I'm prejudiced to the extent that I'm more judgmental of men than of women, and once ended a long-term friendship with a man after a lot of listening because he would not confront the core problem of his life, his wife's meanness. But I am less hard on women, and that discrimination is a fault I suppose.

It leads me to overlook the fact that my father spent one short period during his retirement on a psychiatric ward in Joyce Green Hospital – Dartford had many hospitals, mostly developed before the First World War to house patients from London: imbeciles, lunatics and smallpox victims. This hospital had originally served Londoners recovering from smallpox. They were brought down by barge from central London to an isolation hospital on the Thames riverside and then later taken inland to recuperate at Joyce Green. Smallpox was part of Dartford's collective memory. When in 1962, Wales experienced an outbreak - the last in Britain - my mother hurried me to the Dartford surgery to join the long line for inoculations, a row of maybe twenty people, sleeves rolled up, the nurse working her way down the line.

I visited my father in hospital but if you had asked me what was wrong with him, well, it was *Malingering*. He had already tried to get himself into a council old people's home with the aid of a walking stick, but was thrown out after his probationary period. He had specified elaborate medically-prescribed dietary requirements, weighted towards lean meat, but was then discovered to have large supplies of junk food hoarded in his room. He did like to have his meals cooked for him and Joyce Green did that for you. They turned the tables on him and taught him how to cook as part of his rehab. My rational self would acknowledge some depression, but no more and possibly less than would now be treated by medication. There is also the matter of his eccentricity and how you interpret that. Until the last few years of his retirement, he lived in a static caravan the ground around which became a baroque scrapyard where things of all descriptions from mangles to tricycles waited to be repaired, competing for space with aviary birds, plant seedlings, and decaying objects which might come in useful. Indoors, old newspapers piled up and hoarded yogurt pots pushed open the doors of cupboards. There was really nowhere to sit down.

He took it badly when his live-out partner Betty, an independent and wealthy woman ten years younger, told him when he reached seventy that she wanted to end their sexual relationship. He went to her house, raging against the dying of the light, and threw stones at the lamps illuminating her porch, something for which I find myself giving him credit. She did too, because she continued to care for him until his death fifteen years later and even though his querulousness made it a very stressful commitment. After his intestate death, she handed over a tin box in which he had hoarded many thousands of pounds. When he lived in the caravan, the outdoor steps were propped up by an old and seemingly disused metal safe. But the money was kept there, in plain view if you like. When in his early eighties he was moved into sheltered accommodation, she persuaded him to entrust her with safe keeping of the tin box. I did not know of its existence. I opened it in front of Betty and my two daughters, who had gone with me to her house. I laughed, displayed the contents, pulled out three fifties and handed them out and later made a proper distribution: accounts for my daughters maturing on their eighteenth birthdays and a cheque for Betty with a covering letter urging her to blow it on a holiday. She had taken the brunt of my father's decline and she needed one.

*

My mother had many stones cast at her, from *You wicked girl!* through my father's abuse and on to my own teenage contributions. But somehow I learnt to withhold judgment, at least in relation to women, sometimes not bother with it at all. What do we gain anyway? In the past, women confided because I listened. It's true, I sometimes sought out those with secrets they needed to tell. The desire to hear stories was not with the aim of doing anything with what I was going to be told, just to feel a bit more at home. But for some of us, home is a far country and, whatever we do, we are always a long way away. The trains are late, the roads congested, the route in any case unclear. And there is nowhere else to go. The stories weren't always the ones which modern political correctness likes to hear and sometimes that was part of the problem: who can you tell when you fear the modern versions of *You wicked girl!* But everyone has their Satanic moments, a truth which zealots of all persuasions, ancient and modern, will never concede because it implies that they too are all too human. Allow yourself to acknowledge that, and you might hesitate over the anathema you are about to pronounce. Meanwhile, I keep the secrets and loathe the zealots.

*

My mother was born Hilda May Stevens the 17th May 1907 and died Hilda May Pateman the 10th June 1978. She had never agreed to a divorce; her husband sent to her cremation a wreath of red roses from his garden, and then outlived her by many years. My life has its opening date and then its troubles, successes, failures, offences, disappointments, periods of contentment, and awaits its closing time. I try to think of that other Stevens, Lord Darlington's butler, and want to sit down quietly beside him on Weymouth Pier and listen to his thoughts, just as the lights go on:

> *...for a great many people, the evening is the most enjoyable part of the day. Perhaps, then, there is something to the advice that I should cease looking back so much, that I should adopt a more positive outlook and try to make the best of what remains of my day. After all, what can we gain in forever looking back, and blaming ourselves if our lives have not turned out quite as we might have wished?*

But I still want to interrupt and ask *What if it is someone else's life?*

Three

[postmarked 27 Aug 1963]

Trevor,

You must of felt very big headed to make a decision like you have against me especially as you delayed the letter until after the court case where I agreed to continue paying the £2 per week for your education after hearing your mother was out of work and again on National Assistance, this ties up well with your Bromley ideas.

You as a son have never shown one decent principal towards me, you just kept taking the big gifts for granted even to the last small one of having your watch repaired it means nothing to you

You did not have the principal to keep your promise to see me on the 28th of July when I was going to give you your birthday present which I had already purchased before your birthday and try and talk things over, but no you did not give me the chance.

No you just throw dirty water in my face, that is the last time you will ever do that.

What a declaration of independence for a 16 year old to make against his father.

What you want to do fast is to learn a few basic principals to start out in the world with.

All I hope is that the people who have taught you to hate me will now put there hands in there pockets for what you will require.

I shall watch things very closely and all I had planned for you are now cancelled and so far as I am concerned you are out on a limb and I shall see to it that there is not a stick for you.

I shall appeal against my agreeing to pay for your keep, I see no reason why I should pay £104 a year for a son who has no respect for his Father.

Why not make another big declaration to the effect that you will take a job (oweing to conditions prevailing) and so relive your parents of the financial burden.

I know many a lad who are making great stride at there work and passing there exams while earning, one has even purchased a £140 scooter for cash and good clothes from his own efforts.

Your Father

Four

*Benjamin Streeton at work in the 1930s
second from left*

Mill Girls about 1920. Nellie standing second from left with large necktie, her sister Winnie seated directly in front of her

*My father's parents in the early 1950s on a visit
to one of their children*

My mother's parents at home about 1920

*My mother's brother Tom on the streets of
La Paz in the 1930s*

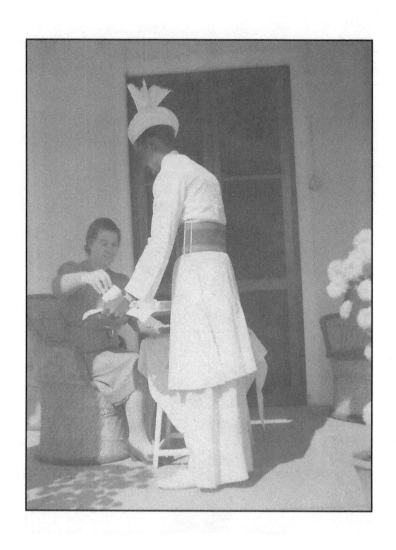

Queenie at home in the 1940s

My parents on their Somerset honeymoon in 1938

Mother and son 1947

Five

THE main body of the text was drafted in 2017-18, relying on memory but incorporating some previously published material and making free use of internet sources in ways which are often indicated. I only attribute actual words (indicated by italics) when I am reasonably confident that something very close to those words was actually spoken. After I had got the first draft into some kind of shape for my editor, I went into what I call the Archive, the large cabinet of documents and photographs accumulated from several people's lifetimes, seeking to corroborate and expand. In this way, I recovered earlier attempts at autobiography. These enabled me to add details and make corrections. I added a few thousand words to the text from things I found in the box files.

I am a bit afraid of the files. I dip into them from time to time, which is how I found the two letters with which I open. It was harder to make myself do the more systematic search, and there are still many things I have not read including my own letters to my mother and hers to me. But it was during this search that I found my father's 1963 letter, which I had remembered as nasty but short. That provided the biggest emotional upset, a bit like encountering the ghost-statue of the *Commendatore* in Mozart's *Don Giovanni* – even though I can see that this commander is not doing his cause much good. Since most of the text had already been written, I decided to create section Three to house the letter.

*

Modern technology makes it possible to include black and white photographs in the body of the text rather than separated out onto gloss paper inserts, and at no extra cost. I looked at some recent books which realise the possibility

- Philippe Sands *East West Street* and Rebecca Stott *In the Days of Rain,* among others - and mocked up a version which did the same. I didn't like it. I thought of two short books which have meant a lot to me: *L'Amant* (*The Lover*) by Marguerite Duras and *La Chambre Claire* (*Camera Lucida*) by Roland Barthes. One is a lyric text, the other a book of mourning. In the original version of *L'Amant*, Duras does not reproduce a photograph of her lover – after all, it's a novel. Posthumous editions sometimes include one. Barthes discusses at some length a photograph of his mother which he is looking at, but it is not among the photographs reproduced in his text, deliberately so. Eventually, I compromised. The main body of the text remains as originally imagined and written, photographs mentioned but not shown. Instead, section Four houses a small photo gallery.

*

Sîan Rees acted as my editor for three earlier books and urged me to write a connected memoir rather than the disconnected autobiographical fragments which they included. So I have done it and once again I am most grateful for her help and encouragement. Fern Horsfield-Schonhut and Sue Atkinson (for the Literary Consultancy) each read a draft and I made changes in response. Jane Ryder in Australia and Jane Stevens in Kent contacted me in the course of doing family histories, and provided helpful information. Louise Griffith allowed me to use the photograph she took inside the abandoned Stone House hospital. Ilva Kalnberza converted my ideas for the book jacket into the version you can now see. Geoff Fisher once again did the typesetting, putting up with my fussiness. I am grateful to each of them.

The colour scheme for the binding is my own. I was tempted to allude to one of the pairings figured in this book, but which pair? I did not want to make that choice and instead chose the twilight colours:

When philosophy paints its grey on grey, a form of life has become old and by means of grey on grey it cannot be rejuvenated, only known. The owl of Minerva flies only when night is falling.

Notes

Notes

page 5: *My Anglican christening* was performed on 24th August 1947 at St. Augustine Church, Slade Green, Richard Agg the officiating priest.

pages 9: *Sister Gantry.* Mary Violet Gantry SRN SCM MTD 1907-1985.

page 27: *Where I'm reading from* borrows the title of a book by Tim Parks (2014).

page 27: *English Folk-Songs for Schools* by Sabine Baring-Gould and Cecil J Sharp was reprinted many times in editions dating from the 1900s into the 1950s.

page 28: *The rich man in his castle.* This is the third verse in *All things bright and beautiful* written by Mrs Cecil Alexander and included in her *Hymns for Little Children* (1848).

page 31: *a horse's head in someone's bed* owes to a line in Catatonia's *I Am The Mob* (1998).

page 34: *Sons and Lovers* was published in 1913; Lawrence was born in 1885. In my secondary school, sixth formers took a two-year course called General English in addition to their A level subjects. We were set novels to read and also took turns to give talks on books of our own choice. I read *Sons and Lovers* at sixteen as a set text.

page 41: *George Lofts.* I went online to supplement my memory; there are only a few references and the most detailed report is to be found in *The Singapore Free Press* 16 January 1957, made available digitally by the government of Singapore.

page 54: *a debate at the Oxford Union* televised live on 23rd November 1967, *That this House believes that the Roman Catholic church has no place in the twentieth century.* Proposed by Mr. Trevor Pateman, St.Peter's, seconded by the Rev. Dr. Ian Paisley. Opposed by Miss Daphne Triggs, St. Hilda's, seconded by Mr. Norman St-John Stevas, M.P.

page 66: *shake your fist.* Edmund Gosse's response to Hardy's *Jude the Obscure* in an 1896 review: *What has Providence done to Mr. Hardy that he should rise up in the arable land of Wessex and shake his fist at his creator?*

page 74: *Brethren.* On growing up in an Exclusive Brethren family in the 1960s, see now Rebecca Stott's prize-winning memoir *In the Days of Rain* (2017). She references Michael Bachelard's *Behind the Exclusive Brethren* (2009) for an extended study and critique.

page 82: John Bowlby, *Attachment and Loss* (in three volumes, 1969 – 1980); Melanie Klein, *Love, Guilt and Reparation*, volume 1 of her *Collected Writings* (1975); Donald Winnicott, *Playing and Reality* (1971).

page 82: *The Mayor of Casterbridge.* The book was published in 1886; Hardy was born in 1840. I am remembering Henchard's testament: *That Elizabeth-Jane Farfrae be not told of my death, or made to grieve on account of me. & that I be not bury'd in consecrated ground. & that no sexton be asked to toll the bell. & that nobody is wished to see my dead body. & that no murners walk behind me at my funeral. & that no flours be planted on my grave. & that no man remember me. To this I put my name. Michael Henchard.*

page 82: *Over Babiy Yar.* The ravine is in Kyiv. Between 1941 and 1943, between 100 000 and 150 000 people were murdered at this site beginning with a massacre of over 30 000 Jews in September 1941. Later victims included gypsies, Soviet Prisoners of War, and Ukrainian nationalists. After the war, Soviet prosecutors pursued the main perpetrators in the Nürnberg trials, but Soviet authorities resisted the memorialisation of the site.

page 85: *self-abasing religious language.* I've always remembered a passage in Michel Foucault's *History of Madness* where he recounts *the cure of a melancholic who believed himself to be already damned on account of the enormity of his sins. As there was no means of convincing him by reasonable argument that he might yet be saved, his delirium was accepted, and an angel dressed in white was made to appear, sword in hand, announcing, after a severe exhortation, the remission of his sins* (page 330 in the 2006 English edition, paraphrasing Observation XLV in Zacatus Lusitanus *Praxis medica admiranda* (1634; the second 1637 edition is accessible free online and the full Latin text can be found there)).

page 88 *happiness writes white.* This is the usual short form for Henry de Montherlant's *Le bonheur écrit à l'encre blanche sure des page blanches.*

page 89: *Joyce Green.* See Nick Black, "The Extraordinary Tale of Dartford, the Hospital Town", *Journal of the Royal Society of Medicine*, 2009, pages 522 – 29.

page 92: *outlived her by many years*. Albert George Pateman 1912-1997.

page 92: *on Weymouth Pier*. Kazuo Ishiguro, *The Remains of the Day* (1989). In the quoted passage, *the advice* is a silent amendment from Ishiguro's *his advice* which refers back to an earlier passage in the text. I am grateful to the author for kind permission to use the passage in this modified form.

page 109: *grey on grey*. From the preface to Hegel's *Philosophy of Right* (1820); my translation.

The Author

TREVOR PATEMAN graduated from Oxford in 1968 with a congratulatory First Class degree in Philosophy, Politics and Economics and continued his studies at University College, London under Richard Wollheim and later with Roland Barthes at the École Pratique des Hautes Études in Paris. His most cited academic work is a study of Chomskyan linguistics, *Language in Mind and Language in Society* (Oxford University Press 1987). He taught for twenty years at the University of Sussex before leaving to become a stamp dealer. In recent years he has published five essay collections including *The Best I Can Do* (2016), *Silence Is So Accurate* (2017) and *Prose Improvements* (2017).

He is father to Isabella and Mitzi; grandfather to Aida, Arben and Oscar Benjamin.